MÍRZÁ 'ALÍ-AKBAR-I-NAKHJAVÁNÍ

WITH NEWLY TRANSLATED TABLETS OF 'ABDU'L-BAHÁ

Mírzá 'Alí-Akbar-i-Na<u>kh</u>javání

With Newly Translated Tablets of 'Abdu'l-Bahá

Ali Nakhjavani

BAHÁ'Í
PUBLISHING TRUST

WILMETTE, ILLINOIS

Bahá'í Publishing Trust
401 Greenleaf Avenue, Wilmette, Illinois 60091

21 20 19 18   4   3   2   1

ISBN 978-0-87743-392-7

Cover design by Jamie Hanrahan
Book design by Patrick Falso

Contents

Acknowledgments

It had always been my wish to write a biography, however brief, of my father, Mírzá 'Alí-Akbar-i-Nakhjavání. I knew he had received many Tablets from the Master, and when I later read some twenty-eight of these addressed to him by 'Abdu'l-Bahá, including a beautiful eulogy in the form of a prayer revealed in his honor, after my father's passing, I felt that even if I was unable to do justice to his services to the Faith, these precious words, at least, should be shared with the friends.

Unfortunately since my many commitments to the Faith took priority, all I could do, over the course of the past decades, as a youth and later as an adult member of the Bahá'í community, was to assemble as much information as I could about his cultural roots, his family, his travels, his services, and his relationship to Tolstoy. Many of these facts my older brother, Jalal, and I had heard from our mother; many I was able to extract from Bahá'í and non-Bahá'í publications as the years went by. And I depended on the research of several other people for this material too, such as Jan Jasion.

Were it not also for the persistence of my grandson, Amir Sam Nakhjavani, such historical details linking my father to the great Russian writer, for example, would not have seen the light of day. I owe great thanks to him, and to all those who helped me fill the file dedicated to Mírzá 'Alí-Akbar-i-Nakhjavání.

Finally, when I was invited to visit the United States for the centenary celebrations of 'Abdu'l-Bahá's visit to the West, I realized that I should put these scattered notes in order so as to give some coherence to my father's story. I was, after all, traveling on his credit card, so to speak! I was following in the footsteps of the man I had been encouraged to emulate since childhood. Perhaps the time had come to share what I had learned of him—this distinguished looking person whose name so few people knew, standing respectfully behind the Master and gazing quietly at them from the old photographs.

The first person who seriously offered to help me in this daunting endeavor was Noemi Robiati. She was kind enough to type up all the notes I had been making and put together my scattered annotations gathered over the years.

She gave these fragments a concrete form for the first time by writing everything up in its historical and logical order.

Then I was given the greatest help by Mark Hellaby, who generously offered to translate, in his excellent and precious style, the Tablets written to my father by the Master. At his own kind and even more important suggestion, Mark also painstakingly researched all the background details embedded in these Tablets and produced lengthy annotations which provide invaluable information on individuals, locations, and events mentioned in them.

But even then, the book in its present form would never have taken shape had it not been for my granddaughter Mary Victoria, without whose sensitivity and respect, talented pen and disciplined mind, all this material could never have been assembled, shaped, and consolidated into the present document. I am also indebted to my daughter, Bahiyyih, for the logistics of getting this little book into print.

These acknowledgments would be incomplete, moreover, were I to omit mentioning all those who encouraged me over the years to write the story of the character and services of Mírzá 'Alí-Akbar-i-Na<u>kh</u>javání. To all of them, and above all to my mother who was the first to tell me of the father I never knew in this life, I owe a great debt of gratitude.

Ali Nakhjavani
Molsheim, France

Mírzá 'Alí-Akbar-i-Nakhjavání

Mírzá 'Alí-Akbar-i-Na<u>kh</u>javání

Family and Early Life

My father, Mírzá 'Alí-Akbar-i-Na<u>kh</u>javání, was born in 1865, in what is now the autonomous Republic of Na<u>kh</u>javán (Nakhichevan). He went on to live and work in Bákú for several years, as well as travel extensively in the Near East. He was also memorably given the opportunity to travel to the United States in the company of 'Abdu'l-Bahá. His life, though cut short at the early age of fifty-five, spanned great changes in his native land, from the burgeoning prosperity of oil-rich Bákú at the start of the twentieth century to the upheavals of the First World War and the Bolshevik Revolution. Throughout these times of transformation my father remained true to his spiritual roots, flexible and forward thinking in his outlook, intellectually curious, and a lover of language and literature. He translated many of the Bahá'í Tablets into Russian, and became a passionate teacher of the Bahá'í Faith, both in his own home and in the regions he visited. Indeed, that new religion would feed his lifelong desire for intellectual investigation and inquiry.

For progress, innovation and inquiry were the order of the day in late nineteenth- and early twentieth-century Caucasia. Like many of his contemporaries, Mírzá 'Alí-Akbar witnessed a revolution of economics and mores in his native land as the development of the oil fields near the Caspian sea, auctioned off to prospectors by the Tsarist authorities, brought technological and social change. The municipalities of Bákú and Na<u>kh</u>javán developed into centers of culture, while Bákú in particular was the powerhouse of a new oil-fired economy, a resolutely modern city that by 1911 produced a fifth of all the crude oil used in the world.[1] In the midst of this crucible of material innovation, the people of Azerbaijan had their own tradition of spiritual and intellectual independence. In order to understand the influences that formed my father's character, it is useful to briefly examine the philosophies espoused by his family and community over the preceding century.

In one of His Tablets, 'Abdu'l-Bahá calls Caucasia the "Land of the Prophets," alluding to its importance to religious history. When He was asked to explain why the Qur'án contained allusions to previous Manifestations but not to Zoroaster, 'Abdu'l-Bahá said that where Muḥammad mentions the "people of Aras," He is referring to Zoroastrians, and that the "Ras" mentioned in the Qur'án is the river "Aras," a reference to Zoroaster Who lived in the area.[2] One of the surahs of the Qur'án begins with the letter Qáf, and 'Abdu'l-Bahá states that this Qáf is a reference to Qafqáz (i.e. Caucasia), shedding light on the spiritual significance of the region.

Nineteenth-century Caucasia was without doubt a hotbed of new religious ideas as well as social innovation. Since the birth of the Shaykhí movement in Iran in the late eighteenth century, thousands of people had been awaiting the Promised One, the return of the Islamic Qá'im who was to bring peace and justice to the world. This messianic movement had spread across the northern borders of Iran into Azerbaijan, and so to the region of Nakhjaván where the first Shaykhí leader, Mullá Ṣádiq, established himself in Urdúbád. Through Mullá Ṣádiq, Shaykhism spread to all of Nakhjaván and to the region of Zangezur, where some 10,000 people are reported to have become followers of Shaykh Aḥmad-i-Aḥsáí. The rest of the population vehemently opposed what they considered to be a heretical sect, while the ensuing unrest prompted the Russian authorities to exile Mullá Ṣádiq Urdúbádí to Warsaw.

After the mullá's departure, another local cleric by the name of Siyyid 'Abdu'l-Karím began promulgating Shaykhí ideas in Urdúbád, teaching of the imminent appearance of the Islamic Qá'im. Bahá'u'lláh, in one of His Tablets known as the Lawḥ-i-Qafqáz (Tablet of the Caucasus), makes reference to this Siyyid, praising his spiritual gifts and insight. Fearful of the commotion engendered by his ideas, the authorities first held 'Abdu'l-Karím prisoner in Bákú and finally, as enthusiasm for Shaykhism continued to grow, exiled him to Smolensk. But they could not contain the movement for long. Soon after losing their beloved leader, the disheartened Shaykhí community in Urdúbád received news that the Báb had declared His Mission in Shíráz, Iran: their Promised One had come.[3]

My paternal grandmother, Balan Duman Ma'ṣúmih, was an early follower of Mullá Ṣádiq and Siyyid 'Abdu'l-Karím. A dynamic woman, she was the first of her family to embrace Shaykhism and later to accept the message of the Báb and Bahá'u'lláh, becoming one of the early Bahá'ís in the community of Urdúbád. Through her, most of her family eventually embraced the Cause.

It is quite extraordinary, given the context of that place and time, to find a woman capable of steadfastly raising her children in a new Faith, without her husband's help and faced with opposition from the surrounding community. The facts speak to her strength of mind and purity of heart, and also in all likelihood to my grandfather's liberality. Mashhadí Ḥusayn Bábayov was a Shí'a Muslim from a distinguished family who may not immediately have shared in his wife's beliefs, but gave her the freedom to follow her own spiritual path. Ma'ṣúmih Khánum's determination in the arena of religion would eventually bear fruit, as her husband became a Bahá'í through the efforts of his own son, Mírzá 'Alí-Akbar.

My father was born into this rather intrepid and unconventional family in the city of Urdúbád. He had one sister, Rubábih, who also became a Bahá'í and married a member of the Urújov family. Like most of the local landowning elite, Mírzá 'Alí-Akbar grew up speaking fluent Persian as well as his own Azeri language, and learned Russian at school. In 1885, as a young man, he entered one of the most prestigious educational establishments in Nakhjaván, where he quickly made friends and distinguished himself in his studies. Muḥammad Khánov, as my father was known, was very talented in several areas and interested in drama and music. Despite the restrictions imposed by the Tsarist regime on his native language, he also loved to speak Azeri, a predilection which was to cause him trouble at school.

During those days, local languages were forbidden at Russian educational establishments in an effort to quash nationalistic movements. But my father, who had inherited his mother's determined personality, did not see why it should be compulsory to speak only Russian in schools that happened to be in Nakhjaván. Very soon, he joined a movement promoting the teaching of Azeri, and became so vehement in his beliefs that he ran afoul of the school authorities, who had him expelled. Although he later wrote a letter asking to be reinstated, his request was denied and he was obliged to leave the students' residence in November, 1885.

At this point, several circumstances came to a head, precipitating the family's departure from Urdúbád. Ma'ṣúmih Khánum decided that in order for her son to have the option of continuing his studies, the family should move to Bákú. From there, Mírzá 'Alí-Akbar went on to attend one or more universities in Russia proper, including an establishment in Tiflis, Georgia.[4] Another factor in their decision was the opposition of local authorities in Urdúbád to the Faith. As Ma'ṣúmih had taken a leading role in Bahá'í activities in her area, she was singled out for criticism and found it expedient to transfer the family's residence to Bákú. She would later encourage other Bahá'í families, especially Bahá'í women, to do the same.

With his university years now behind him and a good mastery of Russian, Mírzá 'Alí-Akbar was able to embark on a project close to his heart, and start translating some of the Bahá'í Writings into Russian. At about this time, he wrote to 'Abdu'l-Bahá regarding his endeavor, and was blessed to receive several Tablets from the Master in return. It was the beginning of many years of fruitful work, which saw my father render unique services to the Faith in the field of languages and literature.

Community in Bákú

Over the second half of the nineteenth century, the foundations of belief laid in Bákú by Siyyid 'Abdu'l-Karím were further strengthened by the arrival of several outstanding Bahá'í teachers in the region. One of these was the distinguished historian Nabíl-i-Zarandí, who traveled to Azerbaijan in 1866 on the instructions of Bahá'u'lláh Himself. Another was Mullá Ṣádiq-i-Bádkúbi'í, a martyr who had embraced the Cause in Qazvín. Bolstered by their efforts, Bahá'í communities grew up in Bákú, Ganja, Bard, Salyan, Geychay, Sheki, and Nakhjaván. Azerbaijan would also produce its own great teachers and defenders of the Cause, contemporaries of my father's youth who demonstrated the independence of mind so typical of their countrymen.

Two such believers were the sons of Mullá Abú-Ṭálib, Ustád 'Alí-Ashraf and Ustád Bálá. These brothers were stonemasons who lent their expertise to 'Abdu'l-Bahá during the construction of the Báb's mausoleum on Mount Carmel; the Master would later name two of the doorways in the finished building after them, in order to commemorate their services. By 1905, as the Faith continued to grow from strength to strength in the Caucuses, these two brothers decided to build a house to provide shelter for believers on their way to and from the Holy Land. But their efforts displeased the local Shí'a clergy, who raised a hue and cry at the construction of a Bahá'í center and incited the population against them. Ustád Bálá, a large and strong man, took it upon himself to move into the new building to protect it from any incursions, thus saving it from destruction.

Ustád Bálá often rescued his fellow-Bahá'ís suffering abuse at the hands of their more fanatical neighbors, and acquired a reputation for responding swiftly to any injustice. When the story of his exploits reached 'Abdu'l-Bahá's ears, the Master responded by referring to him by an epithet that made a play on his name. While Bálá, pronounced with accents on both "a's" signifies "up" in the Persian language, "Balá" without an accent on the first "a" means "calamity." 'Abdu'l-Bahá observed that "Bálá" had become "Balá," as he was "a calamity to the enemies of the Faith."[5]

By the 1880s, the Bahá'í Faith in Azerbaijan was well established, with communities in Bákú and Bálákhány numbering in the hundreds. Some local believers of note were the poet Siyyid Azím Shírvaní (1835–1888), the founder of the national opera Uzeyir Hajibeyov (1885–1948), and Elekber Sabir (1862–1911), to whom we owe a debt for the most reliable reports about the Bahá'ís of the time. Another interesting and colorful member of the Bákú community was the millionaire and oil magnate Músa Naqíov (1849–1919), with whom my father worked for a time.[6]

Naqíov was an important landowner in Bákú, as well as a well-known philanthropist and patron of the arts. It was he who built one of the largest palaces in the city to donate to the Muslim Charity Society, which now houses the Presidium of the Academy of Sciences of Azerbaijan. Another of his gifts to the city was Bákú's largest hospital, built in 1912 and still functioning today as the premises of the Ministry of Health. He was also the main sponsor and trustee of the "Real College," later the Azerbaijan State Economic University.

After finishing his studies, Mírzá 'Alí-Akbar began conducting property transactions for Naqíov, working for several years as his executive secretary.[7] At that time, Naqíov had the privilege of corresponding with 'Abdu'l-Bahá. My father often told the story of how, while prospecting for oil around Bákú, Naqíov invested his own wealth and even entered into business partnerships in the hopes of finding a well, all to no avail. Finally, through the kind offices of pilgrims traveling to the Holy Land, he shared his plight with 'Abdu'l-Bahá and begged Him to pray for divine intercession in his affairs. The Master agreed. Soon afterwards, the right site was found and the oil began to flow. Naqíov was thrilled and full of gratitude to 'Abdu'l-Bahá. He was able to pay off his partners and continued as an independent prospector, becoming very prosperous.[8]

Naqíov once begged the Master to allow him to build a House of Worship in Bákú to parallel the one constructed in 'Ishqábád, a project that met with 'Abdu'l-Bahá's approval. Unfortunately, due to his many financial commitments, Naqíov was unable to carry out this pledge. His failure must have troubled him, for during his last illness he was in significant emotional distress. When Mírzá 'Alí-Akbar, as his trusted friend and advisor, suggested that pilgrims on their way to the Holy Land might ask the Master to pray for his healing, Naqíov is said to have wept.[9] But before the pilgrims could reach the Holy Land on that occasion, he passed away.

By the early years of Shoghi Effendi's Guardianship, there were two National Spiritual Assemblies functioning in the Caucuses, one with its seat in 'Ishqábád and one in Bákú. As far as has been established to date, the Local Spiritual Assembly of Bákú was the only Bahá'í institution to survive during the repressions of the Soviet era, maintaining a point of reference for the community in those difficult years. Unable to hold elections if any one member died or moved away, the members would appoint a replacement from within the community, preserving the operation of that institution throughout the period of Soviet rule.

Just before his untimely death in 1920, my father had a dream that for him signified the fate of the Bahá'í Faith in Bákú. He dreamt that a huge tree with green and fruitful branches had dried up and turned yellow. But the tree did not die, and there were signs of growth at the root. My father understood that this tree was the Cause of God in Azerbaijan and in Russia, which would be banned under the communist regime. Its roots, however, would remain intact, and the Bahá'ís would continue their services.[10] It so happened that when the Universal House of Justice was elected in 1963, the very first contribution it received was a golden ring from the Bahá'ís of Bákú, delivered through one of the Iranian delegates to the First International Convention—a touching reminder that in Bákú, at least, the Faith remained very much alive.

Correspondence and Travel with Isabella Grinevskaya

By the opening years of the twentieth century, Mírzá 'Alí-Akbar had embarked on those particular services which were to distinguish him in the annals of Bahá'í history. Few Bahá'ís at the time were fluent Russian speakers, or able to teach the Faith in that language, while fewer still had my father's understanding or appreciation of Russian arts and literature. Perhaps that was why 'Abdu'l-Bahá assigned him the responsibility of corresponding with two important Russian literary figures of the day: the playwright Isabella Grinevskaya, and Leo Tolstoy, with whom he discussed matters relating to the Faith. It was on

'Abdu'l-Bahá's instructions that Mírzá 'Alí-Akbar began this correspondence, for he would not have presumed to enter into it on his own. In these letters, my father is referred to as "Muḥammad Khánov," and sometimes as "Muḥammad Khánly." He adopted the family name, "Nakhjavání," in later years.

The first person 'Abdu'l-Bahá wished Mírzá 'Alí-Akbar to contact was Isabella Grinevskaya of St. Petersburg, who had written a play about the Báb. News of the Báb's martyrdom and the heroism of His followers had been widely reported in the European press over the preceding decades, inspiring artists such as Sarah Bernhardt and others to commission works on the subject. In 1903, Isabella published a dramatic poem in five acts entitled *The Báb,* which was enthusiastically received and in 1904 played at one of the leading theatres of St. Petersburg. A fellow Russian, Nicolas Zazuline, urged her to publish a similar work based on the life of Bahá'u'lláh. This she did in 1912, again to favorable reviews.[11]

Praise for Isabella's work also came from another eminent literary source: Leo Tolstoy. Wesselitsky writes: "In the summer of that year [1903] the great Russian critic Stassoff visiting Tolstoy in Yasnaia Poliana found him deeply immersed in reading the drama, 'The Báb,' and was charged by him to give his admiring appreciation to its author."[12] In *God Passes By*, Shoghi Effendi refers to Isabella Grinevskaya as a "Russian poetess, member of the Philosophic, Oriental and Bibliological Societies of St. Petersburg." He notes that she "published in 1903 a drama entitled 'The Báb,' which a year later was played in one of the principal theatres of that city, was subsequently given publicity in London, was translated into French in Paris, and into German by the poet Fiedler, was presented again, soon after the Russian Revolution, in the Folk Theatre in Leningrad, and succeeded in arousing the genuine sympathy and interest of the renowned Tolstoy, whose eulogy of the poem was later published in the Russian press."[13]

Isabella recounted of her initial contact with Mírzá 'Alí-Akbar that "I (Isabella Grinevskaya) received one day a letter with the following address: 'To the Author of the book "Báb," Mrs. Isabel Grinevskaya in St Petersburg.' Neither street nor number of the house was marked, yet thanks to the careful postal authorities, that letter, though unregistered, reached me safely." Both the handwriting and signature proved to be unknown, but she relates: "That letter was from 'Alí-Akbar Mamedhanly from Bákú who wrote that he was a believer in the Báb, that he had read in the News of Bákú about my poem, the account of which had interested him greatly and that he would like to get the book. He asked that if he found mistakes against the Teachings of the Báb, could he perhaps point them out?" [14]

Isabella Grinevskaya was delighted to find a genuine believer with whom to correspond regarding her work. A copy was accordingly mailed to Mírzá 'Alí-Akbar, along with her explanation that she had to deviate just a little from the historical facts for the sake of the dramatic whole. She added: "I wrote for a public all unprepared to hear moral, religious and philosophical ideas from the stage; it was accustomed to lighter plays, not a theme about God, of religion, especially about the conception of a new religion, or rather, I would say religion renewed!" [15]

From there, the two struck up a friendship that lasted many years. My father's letters to Isabella about the Bahá'í community in Bákú moved her so deeply that she would always recall the joy she felt "to find that there are in the world people so congenial to one in feeling and in vision." "It was like a star falling from heaven at my feet!" she wrote, "As if I had found a precious stone where I had not expected to find one." [16] By 1911, Isabella indicated her interest in meeting 'Abdu'l-Bahá. The Master decided that it would be best if my father accompanied her on a journey to Egypt, where He was sojourning at the time. After spending two weeks in Ramlih in the company of 'Abdu'l-Bahá, Isabella expressed her wish to become a Bahá'í, and remained involved with the community for the rest of her life.

Correspondence with Leo Tolstoy

As indicated above, it was through Isabella Grinevskaya that Tolstoy learned more about the Bahá'í Faith and began corresponding with my father. In a letter to Isabella, Tolstoy observed: "I have known of the Bábís for a long time and am much interested in their teachings. It seems to me that they have a great future . . . because they have thrown away the artificial superstructures which separate [the religions] from one another and are aiming at uniting all mankind in one religion. . . . And therefore, in that it educates men to brotherhood and equality and to the sacrificing of their sensual desires in God's service, I sympathize with Bábísm with all my heart." [17]

However, Tolstoy's reaction to the Faith was inconsistent, at times full of warm praise and at others more reserved, when some tenet of Bábism or the Bahá'í Faith (he did not distinguish between the two) disagreed with his own views. So at 'Abdu'l-Bahá's behest, Mírzá 'Alí-Akbar began translating the *Tarázát, Ishráqát,* and *Tajallíyát* into Russian for the great writer, to help him form a more rounded opinion of the Bahá'í Faith. In addition to these, my father also translated 'Abdu'l-Bahá's *A Traveller's Narrative* and His text known as *Summons to the East and West.*[18] "Always extend to Count Tolstoy loving and heartfelt greetings," was the Master's advice to Mírzá 'Alí-Akbar, "and treat him with the utmost courtesy, as we are indeed commanded to behave in this way. Perchance he may become fair-minded. There are signs that his attitude hath improved and moderated. It is hoped that, God willing, it may improve further and that he may speak with justice about this Cause."[19]

Unfortunately, only four letters addressed to my father from the Russian philosopher remain extant. Jináb-i-Jazzáb reports that when he met Mírzá 'Alí-Akbar in 'Ishqábád, my father told him: "I have so far received four letters from him (Tolstoy) and in them all he has expressed affection and kindness, combined with praise and appreciation of the Faith."[20] In September 1909, Tolstoy responded to a letter from Mírzá 'Alí-Akbar in the following terms: "I have received your letter and with it the book entitled 'Summons to the Bahá'ís of the East and the West' by 'Abdu'l-Bahá Abbas Effendi. If you have any other books on the subject about which you wrote me, I would be very glad to have them since I am very interested in the teachings of Bahá'ism."[21]

Over the course of those years, he and my father became good friends, so much so that when Tolstoy died in 1910, my father was the one chosen by the Azerbaijan authorities to head a delegation of Azeri public figures to attend the beloved writer's funeral. Certain documents and letters connected with my father (under the name Mírzá 'Alí-Akbar Muḥammad Khánov) remain among the Tolstoy papers in the Bákú archives, to this day. In a letter dated September 22, 1908, Tolstoy thanks my father and tells him that he wishes to write a book on the Bábí religion; on November 28, 1909, he mentions that he has undertaken the translation of a book about the Faith.

Meeting with 'Abdu'l-Bahá and Travels to the West
As stated above, my father encountered 'Abdu'l-Bahá in person for the first time in 1911, on the occasion of his travels to Ramlih with Isabella Grinevskaya. This meeting was to prove transformative and ushered in a new epoch of service for him. Until then, he had only corresponded with the Master; now he had the inestimable opportunity of meeting the Center of the Covenant face to face.

Thanks to his mastery of Russian as well as Persian, my father was a great help to Isabella during that journey, which proved to be so pivotal to her own understanding of the Faith. "The Baháʼís have sent a person from Caucasus who knows my thinking and my language," she wrote in a letter at the time, "to accompany and assist me in my trip. I met this person (Mírzá ʻAlí-Akbar-i-Nakhjavání) in Odessa. He is fully conversant in the Russian language and with him I will undertake my trip to Syria."[22] In fact, Mírzá ʻAlí-Akbar and Isabella Grinevskaya joined ʻAbduʼl-Bahá in Ramlih at an historic juncture, for the Master was about to embark on His own momentous voyage through Europe and North America.

I do not know what it was about my father's personality that so pleased the Master, but it is certain that following that meeting, ʻAbduʼl-Bahá took the opportunity to invite Mírzá ʻAlí-Akbar to accompany Him on His journeys to the West. My father was able to join ʻAbduʼl-Baháʼs party in June 1912, while the Master was in New York, and traveled with Him through a number of American states and cities.[23] Perhaps ʻAbduʼl-Bahá invited my father along for the sake of diversity, for in one of His talks, the Master pointed out that His meetings were attended by people from North America, Europe, Persia, and Caucasia. The only person from Caucasia was my father. The story also goes that while Mírzá ʻAlí-Akbar spoke fluent Persian, he spoke it with an Azeri accent, which is delightful to the ear of Persians. ʻAbduʼl-Bahá, when alone with members of His retinue, would ask him to speak on any subject he chose, simply in order to listen to the accent.

We can only guess at the effect of that historic journey on my father, as he did not leave any personal impressions, restricting his written accounts to notes on the talks of ʻAbduʼl-Bahá. Maḥmúd in his diary makes various references to Mírzá ʻAlí-Akbar's joy at being able to accompany ʻAbduʼl-Bahá,[24] as well as to the various cities they visited,[25] including London and Paris, in the company of such well-known believers as Dr. Zia Baghdádí, Luṭfuʼlláh Ḥakím, and Fujita.[26] But while Maḥmúd noted the details of the trains, steamers, and houses where ʻAbduʼl-Bahá stayed, giving a narrative of what He said as well as what He did, my father recorded only extracts of ʻAbduʼl-Baháʼs talks with a brief preamble about where and when He had spoken. With regard to the content of the talks, the two accounts are very similar, with small details included by my father which are left out in Maḥmúd's diary, and vice versa.

Certainly, those days must have inspired my father to become an ardent lover of the Faith, for following his return he made use of every opportunity to promulgate the Cause. A letter written to 'Abdu'l-Bahá from a biblical scholar and ordained priest in Oxford gives us a glimpse of my father's passion for teaching: "I thank you also with all my heart, for empowering the admirable Mírzá 'Alí-Akbar to help me in my search for Truth. He has been, and is, of great service to me and I shall express my gratitude to him both in private and in public."[27]

Travels to Central Asia

After returning from America, Mírzá 'Alí-Akbar was inspired to continue his travels and, on 'Abdu'l-Bahá's direction, visited various countries in central Asia in order to teach the Faith. On the eve of my father's departure for Constantinople, 'Abdu'l-Bahá addressed him with the following stirring words:

Thou hast been with me for a long time, and I have grown to love thee very much. When I love people I do not tell them to their faces. You know how much I love Mírzá Abu'l-Faḍl and Ḥájí Mírzá Haydar-'Alí, but I have seldom told them to their faces. I am sending thee away. Thou art not alone. The hosts of the Supreme Concourse are with thee. They will assist thee and reinforce thee under all conditions. Doctors tell me I must completely rest. . . . When I hear good news from the believers, then my health is improved. Now if thou longest to see me in good condition, go away and serve the Cause and instruct the souls. The news of thy spiritual conquest will make me well. Wherever thou goest, announce the wonderful Bahá'í greeting to the teachers of the Cause, and tell them on my behalf: *"The responsibility of the steady progress of the Cause depends upon you! You are physicians of the sick body of the world of humanity!* You must not stay away from anywhere for a long time. Travel ye from land to land like the Apostles of Christ, and carry with you the glad tidings of the kingdom of Abhá to the remotest corners of the earth!

Why are ye silent? SHOUT! Why are ye sitting? MOVE! Why are ye quiet? STIR! This is not the day of rest and comfort. Travel ye constantly, and spread far and wide the Teachings of God! Like unto stars arise ye every day from a horizon. Like unto the nightingales, sing every day from a different rose-bush. Like unto the breeze, waft every morning from a garden. Do not stay a long time anywhere.

Let the world profit by your teachings and learn from your examples! My health consists in the progress of the Cause, and *the progress of the Cause depends upon the energy and wisdom of the teachers!*[28]

Mírzá 'Alí-Akbar's subsequent travels covered some 20,000 miles, no small feat in those days. As recorded by Aḥmad Sohrab, he visited Paris; Vienna; Odessa in Russia; Batumi and Tbilisi in Georgia; Gäncä and Bákú in Azerbaijan; 'Ishqábád, Mary, Tejen in Turkmenistan; and Samarqand in Uzbekistan. He returned home by way of 'Ishqábád, Bákú, and Tbilisi, visited Yerevan in Armenia, then Julfá, Marand, and Tabríz in Persia. When 'Abdu'l-Bahá heard all these names He was very pleased, saying: "When the enemies exiled us from Tehran, they were dancing with joy because they thought this Cause will come to an end. From Tehran to Baghdád there were only one or two Bahá'ís. The ruler of Persia gleefully exclaimed that he had uprooted the tree of this Cause. Now consider how in all these places there are so many Bahá'ís."[29]

Marriage and Life in the Holy Land

In those days, marriages were still arranged in the East, and the Iranian friends often turned to 'Abdu'l-Bahá for guidance in matters of matrimony. While 'Abdu'l-Bahá and His retinue were in America, He had told my father and another Bahá'í, Dr. Zia Baghdádi, that He would like to give two girls to them in marriage. He used the word "dukhtar" on that occasion, which has a double meaning in Persian, signifying either "girls" or "daughters." The two men did not know which of the meanings 'Abdu'l-Bahá had in mind.

He was in fact thinking of two sisters, Fáṭimih Khánum and Zínat Khánum,[30] both of whom lived in Haifa. The Master's decision was indicative of His trust in my father and in Dr. Baghdádi, for these young women had been associated with 'Abdu'l-Bahá's family since childhood and had a special place in His heart. Fáṭimih Khánum was the daughter of Ḥusayn Áqá and the granddaughter of 'Alí-'Askar of Tabríz, whose family had joined Bahá'u'lláh in Adrianople and accompanied Him on His exile to 'Akká. She was greatly loved by 'Abdu'l-Bahá, not only because of her family's loyalty but also because of her own special services in the household as a personal maid to the Greatest Holy Leaf.

Any discussion of the circumstances surrounding Fáṭimih Khánum's marriage would be impossible without understanding something of her individual experience and personality. She had waited on Bahíyyíh Khánum since the age of nine, in the very room that housed the sacred remains of the Báb before they were transferred to Haifa, then interred on Mount Carmel. She was the essence of discretion and self-effacement, brought up in an environment which was to all intents and purposes a hallowed setting, with no division between the private and the sacred. An insight into her circumstances may be obtained from the story of how she first laid eyes on my father.

One and a half years after the memorable trip to America, 'Abdu'l-Bahá received Mírzá 'Alí-Akbar at His home in Haifa in the days preceding the planned wedding. On that occasion, the Master asked Bahíyyíh Khánum to let Fáṭimih Khánum know that the gentleman He had chosen for her had arrived. Since Eastern men and women still met separately in those days, Bahíyyíh Khánum took my mother to a room adjoining the one in which the Bahá'í meetings (*majlis*) took place, and directed her to look through the keyhole at the gathering, where my father was present. That was Fáṭimih Khánum's first glimpse of her future husband.

This seems strange to us, a century later. What about the choice of the two parties? Didn't they have a say in the marriage? What about parental consent? But 'Abdu'l-Bahá loved certain people to such an extent that He knew they had no wish but His wish, and trusted Him to do what was best for them. This was a society based on arranged marriages, and in that sense 'Abdu'l-Bahá fulfilled the role of a surrogate parent. Everyone was happy with the plan; the wedding of Mírzá 'Alí-Akbar and Fáṭimih Khánum took place on Naw-Rúz Day in 1914, at the Master's House.

For some months following his marriage, Mírzá 'Alí-Akbar rented a home in Haifa where he distinguished himself by his magnanimous nature and generosity toward the community, underwriting the costs of some of the Bahá'í feasts for the friends. Two years later he also asked Mírzá Muhsin Afnán, the son-in-law of 'Abdu'l-Bahá, to find him a suitable property for purchase in Haifa. Their correspondence shows that Mírzá Muhsin found land worth 4000 Manat (roubles),[31] which Mírzá 'Alí-Akbar acquired. This land was later donated to the Faith by his heirs and eventually became the property of the Universal House of Justice.

Return to Bákú
My father's marriage signaled the start of an all-too-brief period of domestic happiness. After almost two years spent away from his homeland and several months living in Haifa, Mírzá 'Alí-Akbar finally settled down in his native Azerbaijan in 1914, accompanied by his new bride. They lived in Bákú, where they occupied a flat on the first floor of a building owned by my father,

just opposite the Baháʼí center at that time. My father also owned a country residence outside the town, as well as land that had been set aside for oil prospecting.

Mírzá ʻAlí-Akbar was a cultured man, and during these few years was able to introduce Fáṭimih Khánum to a very different life than the one she had known in Haifa. He treated her as he felt a lady ought to be treated, and took her to the new opera house that had recently been constructed in Bákú, buying her a pair of mother-of-pearl binoculars with which to view the productions. Sadly, their happiness was short-lived, interrupted by ongoing illness and the worsening political situation in Azerbaijan.

For by the time of the collapse of the Russian Empire during the First World War, there were already signs of the internecine violence that would tear the region apart in years to come. Shortly after the Bolshevik Revolution, traditionally Azeri territory became part of the Transcaucasian Democratic Federative Republic, which included Georgia and Armenia. This arrangement quickly deteriorated, however, as armed conflict escalated in the region, resulting in the declaration of an independent Azerbaijani Democratic Republic in May 1918. Bákú was the scene of devastating ethnic massacres, while the threat of revolution and Soviet incursion only intensified.[32]

Against this backdrop of larger conflict and chaos, two personal tragedies affected my parents. The first was the death of their eldest son, born toward the beginning of their marriage, who died in infancy. The second concern was my father's health, which had begun to fail and worsened considerably toward 1919–20. In the last years of their marriage, the couple had two more children: my older brother Jalal, who grew up to be a Baháʼí pioneer in Africa and Europe, and who passed away in 1982, and myself. Mírzá ʻAlí-Akbar succumbed to his final illness before I was born.

Due to my father's deteriorating health, the family moved to their country house in the last months of his life, both in order to escape the situation in Bákú and also in an effort to find peaceful surroundings where he could convalesce.[33] My father was a diabetic and had a weak heart, and no suitable treatments were available for those illnesses in Azerbaijan at the time. He passed away on December 31, 1920, on the eve of the Communist revolution in Azerbaijan, at the age of just fifty-five.

Alone and bereft after her husband's death, Fáṭimih Khánum sought ʻAbduʼl-Baháʼs advice. He directed her to return to Haifa with her two small children, where she would always be assured of a home. The family traveled to Constantinople in 1921, but were met there by the heartbreaking news that ʿAbdu'l-Bahá had also passed away.[34] Such was Fáṭimih Khánum's discretion that she immediately put her own plans on hold and stayed where she was, waiting to see whether Shoghi Effendi would wish her to complete her journey. After he reiterated his Grandfather's invitation, Fáṭimih Khánum continued on to Haifa. She would spend many years living in the Holy Land under the protection of the Guardian, who took a special interest in the education of her two boys.

After the collapse of the Soviet Union in 1991 and Azerbaijan's renewed independence, my wife was able to visit the country in the company of Amatu'l-Bahá Rúḥíyyih Khánum. On that occasion, the local Baháʾís told her that my mother had felt it unwise to carry my father's private papers and documents with her out of the country, and instead had distributed them among reliable friends in the hopes of retrieving them later. Unfortunately, the Soviet authorities were known for searching the homes of those they considered a threat to the regime, including the Baháʾís. As the situation in Azerbaijan worsened and the community came under threat, those friends and family members who had been entrusted with my father's papers felt it necessary to destroy anything which could be used by Soviet agents as an excuse for their arrest and conviction. In the course of these events, many and indeed most of my father's personal documents were lost.

Mírzá ʿAlí-Akbar's legacy, however, remains undimmed. He packed an extraordinary amount of activity into his short life, engaging with the intellectuals of his era in a manner which they appreciated and understood. Apart from his letters to Leo Tolstoy and Isabella Grinevskaya, he carried out a varied correspondence with several other Russian-speaking writers of his day, in Bákú and elsewhere. Historians record his significant contributions to Azeri culture; he was a member of the local literature society, and even began writing an allegorical fiction of his own toward the end of his life which he translated into Russian. Poetry was also an important part of Mírzá ʿAlí-Akbar's repertoire, and a poem he wrote in the Azeri language, composed on the occasion of a memorial meeting held in honor of Mullá Ṣádiq-i-Bádkúbi'í, is still extant. His life experiences were largely unparalleled for someone of his generation in Azerbaijan, where he is remembered to this day with love and respect. His grave lies within the main cemetery in Bákú.

Attitudes and Perspectives of my Father

When describing our father to us, my mother told Jalal and I that he had adopted certain spiritual habits and practices that helped mold his character and made him the outstanding Bahá'í that he was.

One was his dedication to the Covenant. For my father, the very heart of spiritual life was absolute fidelity to this foundation stone of God's glorious Cause. The Center of the Covenant was, of course, 'Abdu'l-Bahá, and it was He Who exemplified the spirit of service. My mother told us that our father made every effort to pattern his life after the Master's shining example, and that we should do the same.

She told us that, like him, we should use 'Abdu'l-Bahá's method of promulgating the teachings of the Faith through the presentation of core principles, such as the independent investigation of truth, the harmony between science and religion, and so on.

Furthermore, if we wished Bahá'u'lláh to use us as tools for establishing peace in the world, we needed to be united among ourselves. Criticism of others, backbiting, disputations, and differences should be avoided. If we made a mistake, we should apologize to those affected as soon as possible; if such action was not taken immediately, it would become like a piece of stale bread, and be hard to swallow.

My mother told us that like the outstanding Bahá'ís of Bákú, we should serve the Cause with courage, enthusiasm, and detachment. She urged us to follow the example set by Mullá Ṣádiq-i-Bádkúbi'í, whose audacity and zeal led to his martyrdom in Bákú. There was a difference, she said, between faith and love. When one accepted the Faith, one joined the community of believers—but when one developed one's spiritual capacities further, one became an ardent lover of the Cause.

My father had the habit of carrying a small notebook with him, in which he wrote in his own hand a selection of Bahá'í prayers. To him prayer was, as Bahá'u'lláh affirmed, a ladder for souls to ascend to the Kingdom on High. My father always kept that ladder with him.

Tablets and Letters
Addressed to Mírzá 'Alí-Akbar-i-Na<u>kh</u>javání and Other Believers in Bákú

TABLETS OF 'ABDU'L-BAHÁ

1

He is God.

O thou who art steadfast in the love of God! It is some time since I wrote a letter; yet at all times I have been fervently pleading at the Threshold of One-ness that thou mayest in all thine affairs become the embodiment of God's bountiful favours, mayest with heart and soul expend thyself in the path of the Omnipotent One, and mayest occupy thyself with rendering services to Áqá Músá,[1] enabling his mind to be at rest.

Praise be to God, thou art assisted and confirmed, for he is to the utmost degree satisfied with thee, while his contentment is a source of happiness to the hearts of all, especially at this time when he hath been assailed by tests; yet praise be to God, despite such trials he remaineth patient and steadfast, and I fain would hope that, through the grace of the Almighty, his peace and composure may reach the point of perfection. For during the past year, Divine tests assailed everyone with the utmost severity and intensity; yet, through the help and favour of the True One, the friends all made firm their steps and evinced a prodigious steadfastness. Wherefore it is my hope that, by the leave of God, Áqá Músá will provide the friends with a goodly example, and one which, in occasions of adversity, they will all emulate.

A prayer hath been composed beseeching forgiveness for his late lamented son, who ascended unto a seat of truth:[2] thou must recite it, making clear and evident its purport.

Greeting and praise be upon thee.

2

He is God.

O thou servant of the kindly Beloved, Baháʾuʾlláh! I can find no nobler title than this wherewith to address thee. Only an hour ago I wrote thee a letter; and now, as I was sorting through my papers, the portrait of that loving friend fell out. When I beheld that adorable countenance, I bestirred myself again to write this present letter, in order that thou mightest know how dearly thou art cherished in these precincts. I fain would hope that at all times, through the grace and bestowals of the Blessed Beauty, that countenance may, through the lights of Divine confirmation, become the envy of the radiant moon, and be brightened and illumined by the rays of the Sun of Truth.

The Glory of Glories rest upon thee.

Shouldst thou be able to convince that Armenian gentleman[1] to write the truth, and himself repudiate what he hath written—which is utter falsehood and pure calumny—it would be most agreeable. Exert thou the utmost effort in this regard.

3

He is God.

O thou who art steadfast in the Covenant! Thou didst trace a design for a Bahá'í emblem. It is wondrously well done! Yet the badge of the Bahá'ís must be such conduct, deeds, and manners as are in conformity with the teachings of Bahá'u'lláh. This is the emblem of Him Who is the Traceless, the Brilliant Orb of the heavenly world.

Thou didst write concerning the Spiritual Assembly. Should I write aught, it would be a cause of sorrow to some. Wherefore do thou in an agreeable fashion endeavour that the Spiritual Assembly may be organized. This is the better way.

As for Count Tolstoy, when once that Armenian person[1] hath, thanks to thine endeavours, corrected his errors in his book, send thou a copy thereof to Count Tolstoy. It would be difficult, however, for Tolstoy to accept this Cause, for his aspiration is to be the unique and peerless figure of the age amongst men. In view of this prepossession and determination on his part, it would be most difficult for him to recognize the advent of a Universal Manifestation from the Dayspring of Divine Unity during his days. Rest thou assured, however, that erelong thousands like unto Count Tolstoy will be gathered beneath the shadow of the banner of the one true God.

Deliver to all the friends a most wondrous Abhá greeting.

The Glory of Glories rest upon thee.

Shouldst thou be successful in inducing that Armenian himself to repudiate his words, confessing that certain self-interested persons had misled him, it would be most agreeable, for, as thou hast observed, that which he hath written is utter calumny and sheer misrepresentation on the part of the Covenant-breakers.

4

He is God.

O thou herald of the Covenant and Testament! Thy numerous letters have been received, and the contents of all were a cause of joy and gladness. Praise be to God that thou hast been thus aided and confirmed to render service, and hast arisen in such a manner to evince thy servitude to the Sacred Threshold. This is an abiding sovereignty, this is a perpetual bestowal! The response to thy missives hath been delayed, a delay occasioned by the severe disruptions, numerous preoccupations, and pressing concerns—among them the impending journey—leaving no opportunity to attend to the matter.

Now, since I have arrived from Haifa at Port Said—there being a surpassing wisdom in this journey, which shall be revealed hereafter—I am writing a brief response; God willing, I shall respond more fully later.

Convey to all the beloved of God a most wondrous Abhá greeting, saying: "O friends! The time hath come for you to devote yourselves with all your powers to the service of the Cause of God, to arise to spread abroad the sweet savours of God, and to make such a joyful noise that Caucasia—nay the whole of Russia—will be stirred into motion."

ʻAbdu'l-Bahá hath with all his soul dedicated himself to sacrificial service: He cherisheth the hope of expending himself in this endeavour a hundred times more devotedly than heretofore, and each day longeth to hasten unto the field of martyrdom. The friends too must, in this service and endeavour, be my comrades and companions, my partners and peers: most especially Mírzá ʻAlí-Akbar, who, with a godly power and a heavenly resolve, must sacrifice himself in the path of the Lord.

The Glory of Glories rest upon thee.

Kindly deliver on my behalf to his honour Shaykh ʻAlí-Akbar[1] the following message: "Time and again we suffered exile and banishment; for thee too a draught from this cup is needful, and a share of this most great bestowal is requisite, for thou art deserving of this bestowal and bounty." The Glory of Glories rest upon him.

5

He is God.

O thou who art dear to 'Abdu'l-Bahá! Thy letter was received, and the report of Count Tolstoy was also perused. In truth, it is thanks to thine endeavours that the Count hath become more fair-minded, completely abandoning his former partiality. I hope that in all instances thou wilt be confirmed and assisted in rendering service to the Abhá Threshold—may my life be a sacrifice to His loved ones—and that thou wilt correspond with the aforesaid Count. It would do no harm to send him the translation of certain Tablets that are appropriate to his circumstances and agreeable to his taste: yet not in such a manner that the Russian state would suspect that thou art in agreement and concert with him in all principles—even that of involvement in political affairs, for the aforesaid Count is extremely involved in political affairs.

Thou didst write concerning the Russian lady:[1] thou hast permission to come with her on a visit hither. I hope that in this journey thou wilt be blessed with the gracious favours and loving-kindness of Him Who is the All-Glorious, the Most Great.

When once thou hast rendered the Hidden Words into Russian, shouldst thou print this, it would be most acceptable; and shouldst thou also translate *Some Answered Questions*, that too would be agreeable.

The Glory of Glories rest upon thee.

6

He is God.

O true friend! The letter thou didst send hath been perused. In these last few days we have returned from the territory of the Franks—lovely as a rose garden!—to Alexandria, the homeland of the Copts. Behold "the disparity of the way—from whence we departed, and whither we are come!"[1] The tidings of the steadfastness of the friends, and of their service to the Divine Threshold, was a source of joy and gladness.

Madame Isabella hath truly, in the composition of her book, exerted an extraordinary endeavour. Convey to her on my behalf the utmost good-pleasure and satisfaction. God willing, she will be successful in representing and enacting these two dramas.

Thou hadst requested a teacher of the Cause. None is available in these parts; a message will be sent to Ṭihrán.

As for the Theosophical Society, shouldst thou attend their gatherings and speak of the oneness of humanity; of the contents of the Divine Tablets; of the spirituality born of heaven; and of equality, concord, love, and harmony among the children of men; and consort with them with the utmost attraction, this will doubtless be beneficial.

Gulnár[2] is in Egypt: When I came to Alexandria, she sent a telegram of felicitation on my arrival, and I too wrote her a reply. The thoughts of this lady are slightly distracted.

In fine, in Bákú there is freedom of faiths and religions: If the friends exert an effort, the Faith will be greatly propagated, and the Divine fragrances will stir the people into motion.

That true friend is in truth exerting the utmost industry and diligence that he may render a service to the Sacred Threshold. My hope is that, through the gracious favours of the True One, he may prosper in all his affairs.

7

He is God.

O thou who art steadfast in the Covenant! The letter which thou didst compose after thy return hath arrived. In this journey, the Russian lady was, through the diligent endeavours of that faithful friend, guided unto the pathway of the Beloved.

The first book, she should assuredly correct; if she be successful in this, the harbinger of Divine bounty shall reach her and make of her an illumined candle. Concerning the enactment of her piece, to the extent possible no effort will be spared; thereafter the matter is in the hands of God.

The news of the unity and concord of the friends, and of the fellowship and oneness of Áqá Kíshí[1] and Ustád Áqá Bálá,[2] was a cause of the utmost joy and gladness. I hope that under all conditions thou wilt be assisted and confirmed.

Praise be to God, that Armenian gentleman[3] hath, in the Petersburg newspaper, made good his oversight in respect of what he had written in his first treatise, become apprised of the reality of the matter, and corrected the tenor of his address; and this too is thanks to your diligent endeavours.

Praise be to God, after thine arrival public gatherings were arranged and properly organized in Bákú, and this is as a result of Divine confirmations.

The Glory of Glories rest upon thee.

O thou faithful stalwart! In truth, in the pathway of the Most Great Name, His Holiness the Glory of the heavens and of the earth, thou hast evinced—as thou dost still—the utmost degree of self-sacrificial devotion. Be thou assured of assistance and confirmation.

Praise be to God, thine honesty and trustworthiness are evident and proven in the eyes of Áqá Músá. In fine, in Bákú and Bálá-Khání—nay, throughout the whole of the Caucasus—some effective means must be adopted so that their inhabitants may benefit from the bounties of God and, having escaped from the darkness of waywardness and ignorance, become illumined beings.

If thou art able to establish a school for the youth, wherein, under the tuition of Áqá Shaykh 'Alí-Akbar,[4] they may study how to teach the Cause and become informed of the Divine proofs and testimonies, it would be most agreeable.

Gulnár the Russian[5] arrived in Alexandria, where she met me and experienced some mild spiritual sensations; yet since she was intending to return to Kazan, her thoughts were much preoccupied. She had absolutely no leisure. Do thou communicate with her: Perchance through thy guidance and that of the Russian lady[6] she will little by little be fully awakened.

For the rest, deliver unto each of the friends a most wondrous Abhá greeting; cleave unto that which is the cause of enkindlement and attraction, and hold the Nineteen-Day Feast.

Convey on my behalf to the heavenly Shaykh 'Alí-Akbar the utmost love, devotion, and kindness.

The Glory of Glories rest upon thee.

8

He is God.

O thou who art steadfast in the Covenant! The letter thou didst write hath been perused. Thou didst write concerning the diffusion of the Divine fragrances in that city. This was news such as to uplift the spirit. Assuredly thou hast by now brought together several of the friends, and been successful in dispatching teachers to outlying parts.

Convey to Madame Isabella the Russian my utmost love.

Should Mr. Browne[1] pass through Bákú, do thou assuredly extend to him the utmost love and kindness: Perchance he will forgo his present tendentious course and speak with fairness, for the Azalís have misrepresented the matter in his eyes.

With respect to Isabella's book, I wrote a letter to Paris, but this apparently hath not arrived. I shall write again.

In fine, my hope is that, through God's invisible assistance, thou mayest day by day render ever greater service, and conduct thyself with the utmost steadfastness, so that the Caucasus may become the nest of the phoenix of mystery,[2] Bákú may become redolent of musk, Tiflís may become a precious gem, Ganjih[3] may become a store of riches, and Shíshih[4] may become a scintillating pure crystal.

The debt of Alexandria and Haifa hath been discharged, for the sum hath been received, and the receipts that thou hadst previously requested have been sent.

The Glory of Glories rest upon thee.

9

He is God.

O thou who art steadfast in the Covenant! Thy most recent letter hath arrived from Bákú. Likewise, a missive and accompanying printed composition have been received from Madame Isabella from Paris. From the contents of both letters it became evident that her intention is to stage in Paris a dramatic representation of the Cause of His Holiness the Exalted One. I have written her a letter, which is enclosed. After translating it, kindly send it on to her.

Do thou accord importance to the study of English; and should it be necessary to travel to London, that too is permitted.

Thou didst enquire concerning the deputies to the members of the consultative assembly. The deputies too must be elected by the people; that is, those persons who, after the elected members, have acquired the most number of votes must, with the cognizance of the consultative assembly, be appointed deputies. These matters are at the discretion of the consultative assembly. No one should directly, of his own accord, carry out any matter, even should it be in conformity with the approved constitution of the people and state; rather, it should for the present be carried out with the permission of the Spiritual Assembly, and thereafter through the intermediary of the government.

The Glory of Glories rest upon thee.

10

Bákú

He is God.

O thou who art firm in the Covenant! I am on the verge of setting out towards the West. For this reason I have not leisure to write at length. The speeches delivered in Europe have been collected and corrected—nay more, are in the process of being printed. Shouldst thou translate and publish whichever of these are suitable for the Theosophists, it would do no harm. I shall embark in two days' time. Shouldst thou have an intense yearning to be in attendance, permission is granted thee. Convey to all the beloved of God a most wondrous Abhá greeting.

The Glory of Glories rest upon thee.

11

He is God.

O dear friends of ʿAbduʾl-Bahá! A message hath been sent verbally with Áqá Mírzá ʿAlí-Akbar-i-Na<u>kh</u>javání in a particular regard, which since it is involved, this pen hath not the opportunity to set it all down in writing. In question is the matter of confining the teaching work to Muslims. Ye should by all means treat this matter as important, and conduct yourselves accordingly, inasmuch as there is an all-embracing wisdom in such a course. Otherwise, those territories will become intractable—nay, more inimical than Iran. Ye must act with extreme caution: This is necessary and essential.

The Glory of Glories rest upon you.

12

He is God.

O thou mine intimate and my confidant! In Montreal I could not be more busily occupied. The interactions and discussions during the day, and the nightly conversations, are extensive. Of all places, this is the best. There is a great deal to see, a small glimpse of which may be obtained from the newspapers. With respect to thyself, do thou carry out what I instructed thee. There is no opportunity to write more than this. Send thou the letter of Ahmadov,[1] together with the details of the events that transpired.

13

He is God.

O thou who art steadfast in the Covenant! Thy letter hath arrived, and, for want of opportunity, I am now replying to it in brief.

The formation of a teaching council is most acceptable and beneficial. It is hoped that in days to come the desired outcome will become apparent.

The name of his Holiness the Purest Branch was Mihdí, and at the time of his ascension he was in his eighteenth year. The Leaves, or daughters, of the Blessed Beauty were three in number: the Greatest Holy Leaf, Furúghíyyih Khánum,[1] and Samadíyyih Khánum.[2] The Greatest Holy Leaf was continually engaged in service to His blessed Person; nor had she an hour's respite from her devoted labours. In the inner quarters, the Leaves were occupied with the remembrance of God, and with the exposition of questions relating to the Cause of God. Thus did the hours pass. The mother of 'Abdu'l-Bahá[3] was throughout her life, both night and day, engaged in fervent supplication and remembrance, and occupied with the mention of God and the exposition of religious questions and of proofs in vindication of the True One.

The difference between Bahá'í and other women is that, among the other communities of the East, the women are occupied either with the management of the life of the household, or with the pursuit of pleasure and diversion. Bahá'í women, however, while concerning themselves as far as possible with the ordering of the affairs of life, devote the rest of their time to the exposition of Divine truths and mysteries.

As for the miracles that took place in the war of the children of Israel with the unbelievers, and are recorded in the Holy Bible, these have a figurative meaning and metaphorical interpretations; and yet withal the Bahá'ís do not hold the miracles of the Prophets to have been impossible of performance.

Concerning those souls who were formerly in the circle of Áqá Músá, and have now left it, this was as a result of the coercion and insistence of others. For this reason, allow no unseemly word about Áqá Músá to pass thy lips, but maintain towards him a respectful attitude. Almighty Providence will provide for those souls a source of livelihood, while they for their part must abide by the counsels of the True One and, with respect to Áqá Músá, by no means allow any word expressive of dissatisfaction to pass their lips.

Thou didst request that the questions of Áqá Mírzá Haydar-ʿAlí be printed and disseminated. To print and circulate them among the Baháʾís is permissible; but to do so outside the community is by no means permissible, for this would give rise to universal rancour and enmity. Should the friends, however, commit to memory these facts, verses, and traditions, and, in gatherings, question the ʿulamá about them, then, the latter being unable to deliver a response, the people would become aware.

The friends must not—either with the people in general, or with the ʿulamá—speak in a contentious fashion, but rather they should express themselves with the utmost consideration, kindness, and propriety. Nor must they allow any topic to lead to conflict and altercation, for contentious and polemical speech will never be productive of any useful result, but will rather engender rancour and enmity. Wherefore they should speak with the utmost kindness, self-effacement, humility, and lowliness, nor ever let a harsh word pass their lips, saying instead: "We have no quarrel or dispute with any group of people, nor hold them in contempt, but regard both ourselves and them as servants of the one true God. We are all the fruits of one tree, and grown from the same bough. The only difference is that some are searching for the truth, while others are calm and silent, and occupied with themselves and their own interests."

Do thou have the *Narrative*[4] translated into German.

It is not at present permissible to publish the treatise to the <u>Sh</u>ay<u>kh</u>.[5]

Permission is granted thee to travel with Áqá <u>Sh</u>ay<u>kh</u> ʿAlí-Akbar[6] to Iran.

The Glory of Glories rest upon thee.

14

He is God.

O thou who art steadfast in the Covenant! Thy numerous letters have arrived. God willing, replies will be written to each one of them.

Thou didst write concerning the Russian official. It is evident that, thanks to thine endeavours, he hath become somewhat attracted to the Cause; God willing, he will come little by little to believe in it entirely. Shouldst thou have in thy possession a copy of the *Narrative*, send him thereof however much he wisheth, and write to him that Mírzá Abu'l-Faḍl hath composed a treatise concerning this Cause, which hath been translated, and printed in America.[1] Let him request it of the friends in Paris, and likewise the book *Some Answered Questions*, which hath been rendered into the French and English tongues. If he is able, let him render the *Narrative* into the German tongue and likewise the translation of the Tablets Ṭarázát, Tajallíyát, Kalimát, Bishárát, and Ishráqát. In fine, whatever books there are about this Cause may be found with Mr. Dreyfus[2] in Paris: Let him obtain them from him.

Convey to the Russian lady[3] the utmost loving-kindness on the part of ʻAbdu'l-Bahá, and, so far as thou art able, strive to attract that respected personage to the Divine fragrances; for if once that virtuous matron becometh attracted and assured in faith and certitude, then, through the power of the confirmations of the Blessed Beauty, she will become in Western lands a brilliant candle.

Thou didst write concerning the disturbances in Bákú. Do thou have recourse to the government so that preventive measures may be taken; yet not in any adversarial fashion: rather, in a moderate manner state thou that such is contrary to justice and inimical to fellowship and love among all the subjects of the respected state.

In brief, I found myself exceedingly happy and satisfied with thee for thou hast arisen to serve the Cause of God. My hope is that thou wilt be assisted to perform outstanding services and become a means of exalting the Word of God.

Always extend to Count Tolstoy loving and heartfelt greetings and treat him with the utmost courtesy, as we are indeed commanded to behave in this way. Perchance he may become fair-minded. There are signs that his attitude hath improved and moderated. It is hoped that, God willing, it may improve further and that he may speak with justice about this Cause. It might be beneficial if thou wert to despatch to him, and others like him, the letter of this servant addressed to the believers of the East and the West[4] which is translated and published in Russian.

The Glory of Glories rest upon thee.

15

He is God.

O thou who art steadfast in the Covenant! Thy letter hath arrived, and likewise the power of attorney which thou hadst sent for Áqá Mírzá Muḥsin.[1] He hath gone to Jerusalem. God willing, he will return to 'Akká and take measures to purchase the land for thee.[2]

Should Áqá Músá intend to travel to America, he must assuredly come to the Holy Land, and from here proceed to his destination.

Thou didst write concerning the arrival of <u>Sh</u>ay<u>kh</u> 'Alí-Akbar,[3] saying that this had been instrumental in generating a spirit of attraction. The hope of 'Abdu'l-Bahá is that, through the grace and bounty of the Blessed Beauty, he will raise aloft in that region the banner of "Yá Bahá'u'l-Abhá!", becoming the cause alike of the greater enkindlement of the friends, and the guidance of others. Thou didst write that three Russian persons had accepted the Faith. Erelong shalt thou witness all peoples and kindreds entering beneath the shadow of the tabernacle of the oneness of humanity.

Proceed nevertheless with rendering into Russian, and publishing and disseminating, the *Narrative* only if there is no harm in doing so. Yet shouldst thou translate the Epistle of East and West, and send it to Tolstoy, that would be most agreeable.

Convey to the beloved of God a most wondrous Abhá greeting.

The Glory of Glories rest upon thee.

16

He is God.

O thou who art steadfast in the Covenant! The letter dated the last day of the month of <u>Dh</u>iʼl-Qaʻdih hath arrived, its contents charged with firmness and steadfastness in the Covenant of the Wronged One.

Concerning the correction of the book of that Christian person,[1] shouldst thou be successful in this matter, it would be a great achievement, and a most necessary one. If and when he writeth the book he now hath in mind, let him then bring it with him. Pictures of the sites of ʻAkká have been drawn in America, and printed and disseminated there. We will send thee a copy thereof, so that thou mayest give it to him.

We beseech God graciously to grant a cure to Áqá Músá.

For the rest, convey to all the friends a most wondrous Abhá greeting.

The Glory of Glories rest upon thee.

17

He is God.

O thou who art steadfast in the Covenant! During the days when thou wast present here, and honoured to visit the Sacred Tomb, thou didst raise several questions. No opportunity was found at the time to reply to them; now a brief reply is set forth in writing.

The Mashriqu'l-Adhkár[1] must be sanctified from such matters as fund box and treasury; but if, for the sake of poor relief, a box be set in a special place, there is no objection. This decision resteth with the Universal House of Justice, and the receipts of the poor-box must be expended at the discretion of the House of Justice.

As regards the matter of the "Mahallu'l-Barakih,"[2] this is similar to other companies and is also subject to the decision of the House of Justice. A portion of the accruing interest should be expended upon charitable objects.

The term of service of the members of a consultative assembly, ere the convening of the House of Justice, is five years. When the House of Justice is convened, whatsoever its members deem fit must be obeyed by all.

For the present, members of consultative assemblies are at liberty to resign. When more than half the members of a consultative assembly gather together, they may take counsel together and arrive at a resolution.

The chairman of the consultative assembly enjoyeth the prerogative associated with this position, being entitled to cast two votes.

These matters are according to the principles and standards observed today. When, however, the Universal House of Justice is established, it will deliberate upon all these matters, both large and small, and, according to the exigencies of the time, issue a binding resolution.

Whatever hath been set forth in this sheet is not mandatory: At the present time, the course indicated is merely recommended.

A special letter hath been written to the members of the service council[3] through the intermediary of Áqá 'Abdu'l-Kháliq.[4]

18

He is God.

O spiritual friends! When Jináb-i-Nakhjavání was in this Divine Abode, he requested that letters be written to each one of you. Having now faithfully discharged his commission, he hath freed himself from reproach; yet I for my part am abashed, since, having no leisure, I am unable to write to each of you a separate letter. "Whoever is constrained by circumstances is excused, and exempt from the imputation of neglect."[1] I have accordingly composed a single letter, in which I have mentioned all the spiritual friends.

Ye are all the waves of one sea, the rays of one sun, the flowers of one garden, the lions of one thicket, the birds of one meadow, and the fragrant blossoms of one rose garden: wherefore ye are even as a single soul, and this letter is in reality written to each one of you.

Render thanks unto the grace and bounty of the Abhá Beauty for having lighted such a resplendent candle of unity whereby the human world hath been illumined. Whatsoever flaw there be in our unity and concord proceedeth from our own shortcoming; for otherwise, the outpouring of grace eternal hath gathered all beneath the shadow of a single tabernacle, breathing the breath of life eternal, and causing the fragrance of the oneness of the human world to perfume the nostrils of humankind.

Now, exert ye night and day a mighty effort that ye may become dawning-places of the lights of oneness, and daysprings of the splendours of detachment; and, with unsurpassed affection, so mingle together that the cloud of God's loving providence may rain down its bounties, and the lights of His divine favour may shine forth refulgent. Each night and day, each dusk and dawn, I offer fervent supplications to the Kingdom of Mysteries, entreating Almighty God that ye may under all conditions show forth constancy and steadfastness, fellowship and love.

The Glory of Glories rest upon you.

19

He is God.

O thou Divine youth! Thou hast ever been present in my mind, and at all times am I occupied with thy remembrance. The days of our meeting have not been forgotten. Thy countenance and character are ever before my gaze. From the Kingdom of Signs I entreat for thee Divine confirmations, that day by day thou mayest become happier and sweeter, and mayest delight thy palate with the sweetness of the love of God, becoming a cause of the constancy and steadfastness of the precious friends, so that the tree of life may bear a fruit, and the prayers of ʻAbduʼl-Bahá may produce an effect.

The Glory of Glories rest upon thee.

20

He is God.

O thou who art attracted to the Beauty of God! On this blessed day, the birthday of the Day-Star of the world, the Resplendent Luminary,[1] I thought of thee, and penned this festive greeting in order that the heart and soul of that lover of the countenance of the True One, the Beloved of the world, might be cheered and gladdened.

21

He is God.

O true friend! Thou art ever before mine eyes, and dearly cherished; before my gaze, and highly respected. There is no mightier bond in the world of being than the attachment of the heart. Even a chain of steel hath not the same degree of strength. Praise be to God, that bond between the friends is firm and solid; is binding, capturing, and concentrating the Perspicuous Light; and is day by day becoming firmer and stronger. Wherefore, be thou happy and assured that thou hast an attachment of heart and soul, and that, beneath the shadow of the Omnipotent One, thou art the object of illimitable favours.

Do thou deliver the enclosed letter to Áqá Músá.

22

He is God.

O thou servant of the True One! Sulphur is the fire of the love of God, and mercury is the quicksilver of the ocean of the knowledge of God. Combine then these twin noble elements, and harmonize and unite these twin soundest pillars, and so obtain the Noblest Stone—that is, the Jewel of Jewels, the Ruby of the Mine of the Kingdom—so that thou mayest discover the Most Great Elixir and find the Alchemy of Truth, and, casting it upon the copper and iron of men's souls, transmute them into purest gold.

Seekest thou the Mystery of Alchemy? It is this! Seekest thou the Inestimable Elixir? It is this! Seekest thou the Philosopher's Stone? It is this! While all else besides this is devoid of fruit or consequence, of benefit or useful outcome.

Heed thou my words: Seek thou this Most Great Elixir of the Kingdom!

The Glory of God rest upon thee.

23

He is God.

O thou respected lady![1] Thy letter hath arrived. Thou art right in what thou hast written: It is incumbent upon the Bahá'ís to assist thee, for thou wishest well, and thine intention is to promote the Cause of Bahá'u'lláh. At this time, however, the war and revolution have come to such a pass that it would be impossible, even in Europe, to make the Cause of Bahá'u'lláh the subject of a dramatic spectacle. All peoples and nations are occupied with bloodshed; nay, naught is to be seen but the flame of war, which hath ascended unto the very height of heaven! At such a time no one hath leisure for theatre-going. Should a certain figure be made the subject of a drama—even though he be among the world's most eminent personages—it would have no great attendance; and even should a few people attend it, their thoughts would be preoccupied with news of the war. For this reason, do thou for the time being set about publishing thy composition; the time for staging it will come. Although the Bahá'ís are distracted, and, for the most part, poorly circumstanced—except for a small number who are well endowed—yet assuredly they will lend thee assistance in the publication of thy book.

As for the dramatic representation of this book in the theatres of Europe, this will, in truth, have a considerable impact. In Iran, however, no representation of this kind will have any impact whatsoever. A prolonged period must pass ere Iran acquireth such readiness. For the moment no Bahá'í theatrical representation is possible, for most people are inimical to the Bahá'ís. Such is the frequency with which, night and day, passion plays and theatrical representations of the Imáms and Prophets of old have been staged, indulging in vast exaggeration—angels, for example, are shown descending from heaven—and relating highly embellished tales, that such representations have been reduced to the level of a mere childish sport, and have in consequence absolutely no effect.

I am hopeful that thy book will be staged in Europe, but at a time when safety and security, peace and tranquillity, prevail.

As for the question of the fruit of thy works: The greatest fruit is the good-pleasure of the Almighty, which is the foundation of eternal glory; the second fruit is illumination of heart and soul, which is the greatest Divine bestowal; the third fruit is renown in both the East and the West, which shall shine forth effulgently in times to come; and the fourth fruit is that thy book shall in future be greatly in demand. I beseech for thee the exaltation of the Kingdom, as I entreat for thee likewise heavenly illumination, nearness to the Court of Grandeur, eternal life, and spiritual effulgence.

The Glory of Glories rest upon thee.

24

He is God.

O thou servant of the Sacred Threshold! Thou knowest not what a convulsion there is in these parts! All the people are dismayed and distraught, whilst the townsfolk wander without home or shelter in the mountains and villages; for they are fearful lest the ironclads should of a sudden burst into thunderous action, razing the cities to the ground. In brief, thou art well out of it, and free from all this grim clamour and commotion.

Although, inevitably, there are disturbances in those parts also, yet they cannot be of the same severity as those afflicting these parts; for thou art on the shores of the Caspian Sea, where no state but Russia hath warships, whereas we are on the shores of the Mediterranean Sea, where all states have host upon host of fire-scattering destroyers, and the people are fearful lest they should of a sudden launch an attack.

For our part, however—praise be to God!—we are, under the shadow of the loving providence of the Blessed Beauty, occupied day and night, in the utmost tranquillity and assurance, with the protection of the Sacred Threshold; engaged in the remembrance of God; and transported by the utmost fellowship and love.

I beseech for the beloved of God the help of His grace.

A letter hath been received from Isabella Grinevskaya; please find enclosed both the original and the reply, so that—once having perused them—thou mayest send on the latter. If the respected lady wisheth to print and disseminate her book, then, should the beloved of the Lord provide her with some measure of assistance, and extend to her some degree of support, it would be a source of encouragement and stimulation to her.

People are not all on the same level: Some there are who perform their works solely for the sake of God, desiring for their endeavours no other recompense than to draw nigh unto the Threshold of Grandeur—and this is right and proper; yet others there are who belong to that party which is represented as entreating, "Render unto us on earth a favour, and in the world to come a favour likewise."[1] One must deal with people compassionately, for otherwise matters will become fraught with difficulty.

The Glory of Glories rest upon thee.

25

He is God.

O thou who art steadfast in the Covenant! The news of the ascension of his honour Áqá Músá was a source of grief and sorrow, while the problems caused by his former spouse added further to the despondency thus engendered. That the late Áqá Músá was a Bahá'í is famed throughout the East and West, and known to the government. There is no doubt about the matter. . . .

As for the letters of Áqá Músá that were in the possession of Áqá Mírzá Haydar-'Alí, since a considerable time hath now elapsed, these have been lost.

The journey thou didst wish to undertake to the regions of the Caucasus, and other lands, in order to proclaim the Word of God is a most blessed enterprise. God willing, thou wilt undertake this journey with the utmost enthusiasm and rapture, joy and exhilaration, and become a cause of the exaltation of the Word of God.

The treatise thou hast composed relating the new ideas to the Divine teachings is very good. The "sharing" and "equality," however, which are mentioned in the Divine Teachings denote measures that are undertaken voluntarily;[1] in other words, should anyone of his own free will have mercy on the poor, and with the utmost gladness bestow upon them his wealth, such a person is favoured in the Court of Grandeur. And indeed, many of the loved ones of God have with the utmost joy and gladness bestowed their wealth upon the poor, practising voluntary sharing in the fullest measure—but of their own free will. As for the new thoughts current in some European countries, these have to do with compulsory, not voluntary, dispositions, which are destructive of the body politic, and a cause of chaos and confusion in all lands. By equality and sharing, as set forth in the Divine Teachings, however, is intended those actions which one putteth into effect of his own free will and with a goodly grace; and this is a sign of magnanimity, and a cause of the good ordering of the human world. It would be good if, in the second edition, thou couldst make this point, that the difference lieth in this, that while no one is entitled to covet, or dispose of, the property of others, yet souls who are detached from all save God, for the love of His Beauty have mercy on the poor and expend their substance on the destitute—nay more, with the utmost joy and pleasure bestow their whole wealth, or a part thereof, upon the poor. In other words, in their love for their fellow men they are self-sacrificial, preferring the interests and comfort of the generality of the people to those of a particular group; and this is voluntary, not compulsory, and a sign of magnanimity, not of coercion and violence.

Convey to the well-favoured handmaid of God, Fáṭimih <u>Kh</u>ánum,[2] a most wondrous Abhá greeting. . . .

The Glory of Glories rest upon thee.

4 July 1919

26

He is God.

O thou who art steadfast in the Covenant! A letter was dispatched some days previously, containing a letter written to the spouse of Áqá Músá; a testimony was likewise composed, which was sent as an enclosure. God willing, they will arrive.

Thou didst write that even in times of hardship the friends are still engaged in teaching. Such indeed is the attribute of the well-favoured, and the characteristic of the sincere: that by no obstacle can they be obstructed, nor by any eventuality can they be deprived; nay rather, under the direst constraint and calamity, they continue to promote the teachings of the Kingdom on high, while under the threat of sword and fetter they raise the cry "How blessed are we!" and "How blissful is our lot!"

The vicissitudes of the age encompass friend and foe alike. It is not the fate of mortal man ever to attain unto tranquillity of heart and soul. For this reason, one must not attach importance to the changes and chances of the fleeting days of life; rather, he should arise to perform whatsoever it behoveth and beseemeth him to do, irrespective of whether he be reposing upon a couch of ease or threatened by the sword of his enemy.

Thou didst write concerning the progress of the friends of Bákú, reporting that in all worldly and heavenly respects they have charted a course of advancement and success, becoming one and all distinguished from all other communities.

As for the small number that have fallen a prey to the wicked-doers, this may be accounted for by the consideration that when the fire of sedition is kindled amid the dry jungle, it is inevitable that some verdant trees too will be consumed.

For this reason I wrote previously that the friends must hold aloof from all confessions in political affairs, and conduct themselves in an impartial manner. They should attend the gatherings of no party, nor seek fellowship with any faction. Praise be to God! Through the preservation of the teachings of the Blessed Beauty, in all parts of the world the friends have remained protected and preserved.

On behalf of these few souls who, by chance, have quaffed the cup of martyrdom—and likewise those souls who have suffered financial loss—fervent prayers and supplications were offered at the Threshold of Oneness, that the abundance of God's grace might encompass all, and those souls who chanced to be slain might, in the Court of Oneness, be accounted martyrs. Such is the highest hope of this servant.

Áqá Músá—upon whom be the mercy of God, and His Divine good-pleasure—was not successful, during his lifetime, in founding and instituting in Bákú a Mashriqu'l-Adhkár; and I too, as thou knowest, accepted naught from him. If, however, he had erected this mighty structure, what an influence it would by now have exerted, alike in the kingdoms of earth and heaven!

Now the wealth is fallen into the hands of people who, as thou sayest, he would not have consented should enter his home, and whom he held in the utmost abhorrence. Take heed, then, O men of insight! Gracious God! The wealthy friends exert no endeavour, nor render any service, such is their attachment to these earthly riches. Yet then it chanceth that after death their wealth falleth into the hands of their enemies! These latter feast thereon, and, as the common people say, "recite the Fátiṭih."[1]

Thou and some others had requested permission to come on a visit to the Holy Land. During these days, to come on such a visit would entail much trouble and many difficulties, such that ye might conceivably spend six months on the way. Do ye postpone the time of your visit to another occasion.

The Glory of Glories rest upon thee.

14 July 1919

27

He is God.

O thou my companion! I sent thee a letter written in mine own hand, which assuredly hath by now arrived. Since telegrams from here cannot be received in the Caucasus, the letter was sent care of the friends. Now I am writing again to say that thou art permitted to come hither, and we are awaiting thine arrival. Dr. Ḍíyá,[1] accompanied by the handmaid of God Zínat,[2] arrived here two weeks ago and await thy coming.

Advise all the friends that no one should ever utter any derogatory word with regard to the new faction, all should preserve silence. This is extremely important.

Upon thee rest the Glory of God.

Deliver a most wondrous Abhá greeting to the handmaid of God, Fáṭimih Khánum.[3]

28

*A prayer beseeching forgiveness for him recently ascended unto God, Áqá Mírzá
'Alí-Akbar-i-Nakhjaváni, upon him rest the Glory of God, the Most Glorious*

He is God.

O my God! O Thou Remover of adversities and Dispeller of afflictions!
I, verily, implore Thee, as one beset by trouble imploreth the Almighty and
Most Exalted King; and I beseech Thee, as one burdened with sin beseecheth
the Lord of pardon and forgiveness, Him Who revealeth Himself through
heavenly mercy, saying:

O my beneficent Lord! Verily, Thy servant 'Alí-Akbar hath believed in
Thee and in Thy Signs; hath acknowledged Thine omnipotence and Thy
sovereignty; hath been attracted by the fragrance of Thy sweet savours; hath
become enkindled by the fire of Thy love, even whilst in the flower of life
and the flush of youth; hath proclaimed Thy Name amongst his fellows; hath
supplicated unto Thee with a heart intensely ardent; and hath summoned the
people unto the kingdom of Thy grace, both in the daytime and in the night
season, with a goodly manner, a gracious disposition, and a radiant heart,
and with a breast dilated through the contemplation of Thy most resplendent
signs.

Never, night or day, did he weary of Thy remembrance: His tongue would
sing Thy praise at both dawn and dusk, whilst he was directed towards Thee
and turning his face unto the quarter of Thy grace; and he would call upon
Thee alike with his heart and his tongue, entreating Thy blessings and confirmations, wishing to reach the door of Thy mercy, and seeking to attain
the wellspring of Thy grace. Ever was he thrilled by Thy sweet savours, and
his breast dilated by the sight of Thy signs; and he would recite Thy words,
guide the people unto the way of guidance, summon them unto piety and
righteousness, and nurture them through Thy teachings, which are a light

unto the eyes, a spirit unto the hearts, a boon unto the righteous, and life unto the hearts of the godly.

O my Lord! Verily, this Thy servant ever besought Thee, both privily and openly, and called upon Thee, with heart and tongue alike, saying:

O Lord my God! Long hath been the term of separation, and hard upon me the effect of deprivation! I, verily, yearn for the meads of Thy mercy even as a dove yearneth for a companion in its sylvan bower, wishing to behold Thy beauty in the World of Mysteries and to enjoy Thy pardon and Thy forgiveness in the Realm of Lights.

O Lord my God! I, verily, am athirst; give me then to drink from Twin Gushing Fountains, and cause me to enter the Twin Verdant Gardens.[1] Forgive me my sins and dispel from me my griefs, O Thou Who art the Knower of things unseen!

O my Lord! Lowly am I; ennoble me through admittance into the Kingdom. Poor am I; enrich me from an imperishable treasure in the Divine Realm. Sick am I; heal me of my grievous malady. Cause me to enter Thy Most Exalted Paradise, O my All-Glorious Lord, and leave me not forlorn and lonely. Shelter me within the shelter of Thy Most Great Mercy, and deliver me from these besetting darknesses. Destine for me all good in the world to come, and supply me with Thy gifts and bestowals. Forgive me my sins, and pardon me my trespasses. Purify me from all passions, and cause me to enter into the garden of Thy Oneness with a luminous countenance and a heavenly disposition.

O Lord my God! I, verily, long to meet Thee, and yearn to abide for ever among the Concourse on High.

O my Lord! Disappoint not my hopes, pardon me my misconduct, and make me a sign of Thy bounty in the midst of Paradise, that I may burst into song like the birds upon the branches and, with a blissful conscience, celebrate Thy praise amidst the boughs.

Thou, verily, art the All-Bountiful; Thou, verily, art the Most Compassionate; and Thou, verily, art the Ever-Forgiving, the Ever-Pardoning, the All-Merciful.

25 Dhi'l-Qa'dih 1339[2]

TABLET REVEALED BY 'ABDU'L-BAHÁ FOR THE FRIENDS AND CITY OF BÁKÚ

29

Bákú
For the attention of the beloved of God, upon them rest the Glory of God, the Most Glorious

He is God.

O ye who have quaffed an intoxicating draught from the cup of fidelity to the Covenant! Thanks be to His Holiness the Self-Subsistent that ye are come beneath the shadow of the Mighty Tabernacle, and arrived within the Abhá Paradise, in the Illumined Garden. Ye are transported by the wine of fidelity to the Covenant, and stirred into a tumult by the heat of the fire of the love of God. My hope is that, through the grace and bounties of the Abhá Beauty, ye may become leaders of the free and commanders of the company of the righteous; become a focal centre of the traces of Him Who is the Living, the Self-Subsisting, and a dawning-place of the effulgences of His Holiness, the Object of all knowledge; become signs of Divine Unity and manifestations of Heavenly Detachment; become shining stars and radiant lamps; and so kindle the fire of the love of God in the very summits of the earth and the midmost heart of the world that its flame may spread to all parts and regions, and the sweet savours of holiness may be wafted from the rose-garden of understanding throughout the whole of the Caucasus.

O my God! This is a city wherein the fire of Thy love hath blazed, and the lights of Thy knowledge have shone. Make then its precincts illumined, its environs fragrant, its courts spacious, and its happiness immense, through the light of Thy Divine Unity which shineth from that city in every direction of that region; and make Thou Thy loved ones therein the waves of the sea of Thy oneness, the troops of the hosts of Thy knowledge, the trees of the garden of Thy bestowal, and the fruits of the tree of Thy providence.

Thou, verily, art the All-Bounteous, the Most Exalted.

LETTER OF THE GUARDIAN
TO THE SPIRITUAL ASSEMBLY OF THE
BAHÁ’ÍS OF BÁKÚ, DATED 9 JANUARY 1923

30

Bákú   For the attention of the respected members of the Spiritual Assembly

May my life be a sacrifice for your unity and your arising to serve the Cause of God! Praise be to the Sacred Abhá Beauty that a Spiritual Assembly has with the utmost orderliness and splendour been established in that city, and that its respected members are striving with heart and soul to protect the stronghold of the Cause of God, to strengthen the pillars of consultation, to unite the hearts of the friends, and to order affairs in the finest manner. My hope is that successive confirmations will surround you, and that, through the diligence of the friends, means for the advancement of the Cause of God, and the comfort and spirituality of the friends, will be provided in the most perfect manner.

With regard to the estate of him who hath ascended unto God, the well-favoured and faithful true friend of His Holiness ‘Abdu’l-Bahá, Áqá Mírzá ‘Alí-Akbar-i-Nakhjavání, the members of the Spiritual Assembly must with the utmost diligence set about ordering and administering perfectly its disposition. They should themselves assume control of it, scrupulously taking stock of all the houses and lands left by the deceased, and appointing a special person to protect and manage them, so that, according to the instruction of ‘Abdu’l-Bahá, all the proceeds of the houses and lands may be divided and distributed according to the laws of the Kitáb-i-Aqdas. The Spiritual Assembly must send all the proceeds to this servant in the Holy Land; but all the property, including houses and lands, must be under the absolute control of the Spiritual Assembly of Bákú, and no one should interfere with them in the slightest.

59

That eminent personage was immeasurably dear, and well favoured at the Threshold of Grandeur. There is no doubt that the respected members of the Assembly will exercise the utmost degree of diligence in this regard.

The servant of His Threshold, Shoghi

9 January 1923

LETTER ON BEHALF OF THE GUARDIAN TO THE LOCAL SPIRITUAL ASSEMBLY OF THE BAHÁ'ÍS OF ṬIHRÁN, DATED 25 NOVEMBER 1940

31

Ṭihrán   The sacred Local Spiritual Assembly, may God strengthen its pillars

Pursuant to the most sacred behest of the Guardian of the Cause of God—may our lives be a sacrifice to him—this letter is composed and conveyed on behalf of His Holiness to those Trustees of the Merciful.

With regard to Áqá Jalálu'lláh and Áqá ʿAlíyu'lláh, the two sons of the late Áqá Mírzá ʿAlí-Akbar-i-Nakhjavání, he said:

"In the light of the passing of their mother, who was staunch and steadfast in the Cause of God, and their relation to that illustrious personage who, during the travels of His Holiness ʿAbdu'l-Bahá in Europe and America, was at all times the object of His blessed regard, their welfare must needs be made a matter of solicitude and concern. To the extent possible they should assist and guide them."

Written at his blessed behest,

3 Month of Qawl 97   25 November 1940   Núri'd-Dín Zayn

Reviewed

The servant of His Threshold, Shoghi

EXTRACTS FROM A TABLET OF BAHÁ'U'LLÁH TO THE PEOPLE OF THE CAUCASUS

32

He is God, exalted be He: Wisdom and utterance are His wont.

O people of the Caucasus! Baṭḥá (Mecca) hath flowed with water, and the Supreme Horizon hath been suffused with light! By My life! The countenance of Ḥijáz hath been wreathed in smiles, inasmuch as the Tabernacle of Majesty hath been pitched upon the slopes of Carmel, and the Day-Star of Revelation hath shone forth from the horizon of the Will of God, after the veils of glory had been rent asunder by the finger of Divine omnipotence. . . .

O people of the Caucasus! He that was named 'Abdu'l-Karím[1] came unto you, and announced unto you this Mystery, in remembrance of which men's hearts have been enkindled, and in separation from which their souls have been consumed. He, verily, held fast the cord of Mine allegiance, and clung to the hem of the mercy of His Lord, the Lord of all men. . . .

O people of the Caucasus! Give ear unto the call of this Wronged One! This is that call for the purpose of hearing which the peoples of the world have, from a state of utter nothingness, been brought into existence. . . .

O people of the world! The fruits of the tree of man are justice and fair-mindedness. Should he not be possessed of these fruits, he is fit but for the fire. Pride hath blinded both their outer and their inner vision. The world is in need of two things: order and justice. . . .

'Abdu'l-Karím was an exemplar of this Most Great Revelation. Like unto the breeze of dawn, He blew from the quarter of Divine bounty. He himself was aflame with the fire of love for this Revelation, while a portion of the ocean of understanding had been bestowed upon him. This was a token of God's favour unto him. . . .

O people of the Caucasus! In conclusion of this utterance, We admonish you to observe trustworthiness, piety, chastity, honesty, and fidelity. In this day, and from this time forth, the hosts of God are none other but goodly deeds and a praiseworthy character. Aid ye the True One with these hosts. . . .

FROM THE WRITINGS OF ‘ABDU’L-BAHÁ

33

He is God.

O thou who hast believed in a Beauty that hath shone forth upon all regions! Although, to outward seeming, it is some while since correspondence and communication took place between us, yet mine inmost heart is thrilling with the remembrance of the loved ones of God, is stirring like unto the zephyr, and is surging like unto the mighty deep.

These days, the region of the Caucasus hath acquired an extraordinary receptivity. An effort must needs be exerted so that it may be proven that "Qáf, by the glorious Qur'án"[1] is the nest of the Divine Eastern Phoenix: Haply, the voice of the Símurgh[2] of the Cause of God may be raised from those territories and regions, and the reflection of this luminous mountain fall in effulgence and splendour upon this illimitable expanse.

He said:

Phoenix of Truth! For thee have I yearned!

Yet praiséd be God, from Mount Qáf thou'rt returned![3]

Let it be seen what the power of the outstretched arm of the friends may now accomplish!

The Glory of God rest upon thee.

34

Bákú   The Beloved of God and the Handmaids of the Merciful, the Glory of Glories rest upon them, men and women alike

He is God.

O intimates of the court of the Beloved! O adorers of the countenance of the Beloved! The entire region of Caucasia is regarded as attached to the Araxes River, which in the Qur'án hath been alluded to by the expression "the companions of Ar-Rass."[1] A company of prophets, of whom all record hath been lost, were in ancient times raised up in that clime, and perfumed the world of humanity with the fragrant breaths of the All-Merciful.

Likewise, in more recent times, His Holiness the Exalted One—may my life be a sacrifice to Him—was banished to <u>Ch</u>ihríq and incarcerated within its confines. A savour thereof reached the nostrils of Ḥáfiz of <u>Sh</u>íráz, who recited this couplet:

O zephyr, shouldst thou pass by the banks of the Araxes,
Implant a kiss on the earth of that valley and make fragrant thy breath.

His Holiness Zoroaster too travelled and ministered awhile in those surrounds. The "Kúh-i-Qáf" (Mount Qáf) which is mentioned in the traditions and chronicles is this same Qafqáz (Caucasus). The Iranians believe it to be the shelter of the Símur<u>gh</u>, and the nest of the Eastern Phoenix. The hope is cherished, therefore, that this Phoenix, which hath spread the wings of sanctity over East and West—by which is meant none other but the wondrous Divine Cause—will make its nest and shelter in the Caucasus.

Praise be to God that the friends of Bákú were, throughout these years of war, at peace with all communities, and, in conformity with the Divine teachings, compassionate unto all. They evinced an ebullient enthusiasm in the Cause of God, and were intoxicated and transported by the wine of the Love of God. Now must they roar like the leviathan, make up for the years of war, and, with a rousing anthem and a rapturous refrain, stir that clime into an ecstasy of motion, in order that Divine illumination may so suffuse men's hearts that the rays of oneness may shine forth, the shades of estrangement may be banished, and all communities may mingle happily together—may, in love and amity, shed forth an ineffable sweetness and engender such a tumult of rapture and elation that surrounding countries too will be stirred into an ecstasy of motion.

The Glory of Glories rest upon you—men and women alike.

3 July 1919

Facsimiles of Original Tablets of 'Abdu'l-Bahá and Letters of Shoghi Effendi

هو الله

ای ثابت بر محبّت الهیّه چندی است که نامه‌ئی نگاشتم و بعد در جمیع اوقات عجز و نیاز به درگاه احدیّت در خواستم که در جمیع امور مظهر الطاف موفور گردی و بکان و دل در روز یزدان جانفشانی نمائی و بخدمات جناب لاموسی پردازی و سبب آسایش خاطر او شوی الحمد لله موفّقی و مؤیّد زیرا نهایت رضا از شما دارم و نهایت خشنودی او سبب مرور قلوب کلّ است علی الخصوص در این اوقات که امتحانات احاطه نموده و لله الحمد با وجود این امتحان در صبر و ثبات باقی و بر قرار و از فضل پروردگار امید دارم که به سکون و قرار به درجهٔ کمال رسد زیرا درست است امتحان حق الهیّه در نهایت قوّت و شدّت کلّ را احاطه نمود و احبّای یموت و عنایت حق جمیع قدم راسخ نمودند و استقامت علیهم الله بر فرمودند لهذا رجا از خدا دارم که جناب لاموسی در میان احبّا اسوهٔ حسنه گردند و کل در موارد بلایا ثابتی باشند نمایند منا باقی طلب مغفرت به جهت مشایخ مقدّسهٔ سبیل مرحوم ایشان مرقوم گردید باید شفاعت نمائید و صفح و عفو واسع و آمرزگار فرمائید و

علیک البهاء و الثنا عزّ ع ع

Translation appears on p. 21

Translation appears on p. 22

70

Translation appears on p. 23

Translation appears on p. 24

72

هوالله

ای عزیز عبدالبهآء   نامه شما رسیده   و نقره غراف نولستوی نیز قرائت گردید
فی الحقیقه جهت شما غراف   بنای انصاف   که گذشته   و از رضا نفس ساکنین
نیز آگذشته   امید دارم که در جمیع موارد سکونت عنبریاتی روحی لأحبائه الفدا حاصل آنوقت
و موفق گردیده   و با غراف مذکور مکاتبه نمائید   و در جمیع معانی الواح که مین گمان نمائید
و مطابق ذائق او اگر ارسال دارید بمنیت   ولی نه بنو یکه دولت روس گمان شاید زیرا
که شما در جمیع مبادی حقی در مدا خله با امور سیاست   با ابو معنی و بدو کستانید
غراف مذکور در امور سیاسی مداخله موفور دارد   در خصوص غاظر روحی در قتل آنوقت
بودید   با او اذون حضور به   امید دارم که در این سفر موفق با نای فتح حمله
بنیل اکبر گردید   ترجمه کلمات مکنوز بروی نموده   اگر جناب ... بترجمه سیما
میتولست   واگر چنانچه مفاد حنانت را نیز ترجمه نمائید آن نیز موافق و
علیک البهآء الأبهی   ع ع

Translation appears on p. 25

Translation appears on p. 26

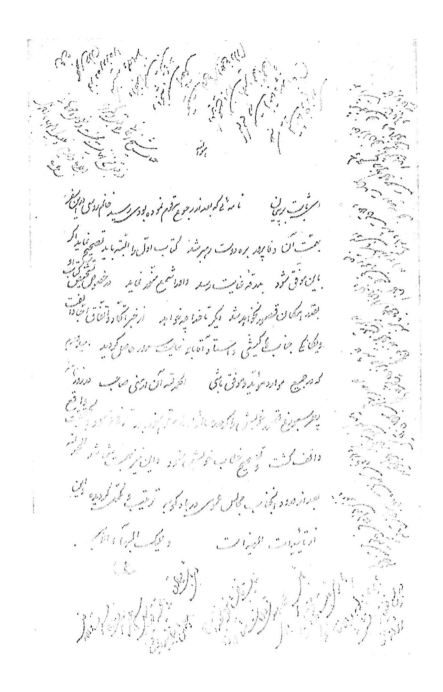

Translation appears on pp. 27–28

هو اسم

اثبات برهان   نامه‌ئی که مرقوم نموده بودید ملاحظه گردید   از انشاء اللّه آیة

در آن مدینه مرقوم نموده بودید   انجر روح پرور بود   دلبستهٔ اکمال چند نفر اتحاد نموده‌اند

و موفق یابان گردیده‌اند که باطراف معینین ارسال نمایند   و بها دوام ابدأ بلا ورسی

نهایت محبت مرا ابلاغ نمائید   اکرستر بزنید   و بکوبه کذر نامه البسته نهایت محبت

و مهربانی باد و محبی دارید   شاید از اعتراف بکذرد   و با انصاف سخن راند زیرا

لحیا بله ما امرا براه مشتبه نموده‌اند   در خصوص کتاب ایزا بلا   بارئیس مرقوم کردهٔ

معلوم است نرسیده   زود به مرئوف مرث   یاری از ثابت بیدار غیبیه الهیه آئیم

چنانست که راز مرور لحظت جسر پردازی   و در نهایت استفاقت حرکت نمائی

تا تفقار اشیاء به عنقای راز کردد   و با کوه مشکو نمود   و تقلیس کوهر نفیس شود

کنج روان یابد و شیشه علوم صاف برمعان کردد   دین اسکندر نیر و خفیا

داده شد زیرا بلغ رسیده قوهنای که از پیش خواسته بودید   ارسالی کردید و علیک

البهآء الأبهی

Translation appears on p. 29

هو الله

Translation appears on p. 30

Translation appears on p. 31

Translation appears on p. 32

Translation appears on p. 33

Translation appears on pp. 34–35

هوالله

ای ثابت بر پیمان   نامه های مستعذ و مثار رسید انشاءالله ملک یک عالی قدری

میشود   از صاحب منصف روسی مرقوم نموده بودید معلوم است که نهایت ثنا خاطر

منتخب کردیده   انشاءالله کم کم لکنی مؤمن خواهد کشت   اگر حافظه کتاب مقال

در نزد ثنا است هر قدر بخواهد نزد او بفرستید   و با و نگارید که جناب میرزا

ابوالفضل رسائلی که در این امر مرقوم نموده   و ترجمه کشته   و در ام لک طبع کرده

در پاریس از احیا بخواهند   و همچنین کتاب مفاوضات را که لسان فرانسه

انگلیسی ترجمه شده   و اگر بتوانند مقاله را بزبان آلمانی ترجمه نمایند   و همچنین ترجمه

الواح طرازات و تجلیات و کلمات و بشارات و اشراقات   خلاق

کینک در این امر است   و در نزد جناب مستر در نفوس در پاریس موجود از انسان

گیرند   و مبادام روسی نهایت هر بار ای از زجل عبدالبهاء ابلاغ دارید فقدار

قوت که رسید که انحصر مرا منتخب ب منفخات الخ کنید   زیرا انتخذره اگر

در ایمان و اتقان انتخاب و اطمینان یاب   از آنا بیات جمال مبارک در

ما لک عزت بثنی روشن گردد   از آن عتشاش باد که مرقوم نموده بودید

حکومت راجحت کنید   ناجلو گیری کرد   ولکن نه منبع عضان طک مستند لا نه

ذکر کنید که این منافی عدالت   و سفارش الفت و محبت در هنا جمیع رعیت

دولت هئیه است   باری از قیام انجناب برخدمت ایران از ثنا سیار

سرور در رضا یا فتم   و امیدم جنالت که بخذمات   فاتقه موفق شوی و سبب

اعلای کلمات گردی   بغراف توستری همتیه اطهار محبت دارد بطر

قلبه و نهایت احترام محری داریم   اما ین مؤدم ثنا یه چشم انصاف کشا به

از قرآن معلوم میشود که جمال مهنر از بیشین است   قذری اعتدال باید به

لکه انشاءالله من بعد بهتر شود   و متفخانه در این امر سخن راند   ثنا المؤب بعزی

این عبد را از شرق و غرب که طبان روسی ترجمه و طبع کرده دیده   و از محبت او

و امثال او از رسال دارید   ثنا یه مفیده کرد   و علیک البهاء الابهی

ع

Translation appears on pp. 36–37

هوالله

ای ثابت برهان ... نامه شما رسیده و همچنین و کاغذ آن ...
که بجهت آقا میرزا محسن ارسال نموده بودید مقدس رفته لو ...
انشاءالله راجعت بیگانه بماند وبخیریه زمین بجهت شما ...
خواهد نمود جناب آقا موسی اگر خیال امر کتب دارد راه ...
باید یارض مقدس آیند وازارض مقدس لوجه نمایند ازود ...
جناب شیخ علی اکبر مرقوم نموده بودند که بسبب حصول انکسار ...
گردیده ... از فضل و موهبت جمال مبارک امید عبدالبهاء از ... باد ...
کرایشان درانشاءان نظم یابد و بیکار الالهی بلند نمایند و سبب ازدیاد ...
اشتغال احباء دیانت دیگران گردند عنقریب ... مرقوم نموده بود ...
که سه نفر روس را خیال نموده راه ... عنقریب ملاحظه خواهید کرد ...
که جمیع طوائف و ملل درظل خیمه وحدت عالم انسانی ...
درآیند ... بلامثال را بروسی نزد مهر مؤمنان و لطیف وانشاء ...
اقزیز نامه مجری دار ولکن نامه شرق و غرب را اگر ... بهم ...
... ... دیمال نمایند سیما موافق ...
... الهی ... ... ایشان اعلاء دار ...
ع ع

Translation appears on p. 38

هو الله

ای ثابت بر پیمان ... نامهٔ بلیغ دقیقه و معقول بود و ... تحریرات مبسوط در سنخ بر میان ... معلوم بود درخصوص نسخ تصحیح کتاب ا... اگر موفق ب آن شوید موفقیت عظمی است و بسیار لازم است و چون کتاب بکه منظور دارد و چون بنگارد و آن وقت با خود بیاورد ... مواقع آنکار را ادام نگاشته‌اند و طبع و نشر نموده و اینک ... نسخه از آن را از آنجهت ... ارسال مینمایم که با و بدهید و از نظر خواهم ... که مشتاق بجناب ... لاموسی عنایت فرماید دیگر می باد اذا نگاشت ... ابلغ امری ابلاغ دارید و علیک البهاء الابهی علی

Translation appears on p. 39

Translation appears on p. 40

هوالله

ای یاران روحانی   جناب نجرانی   وقتی که در این ایوان یزدانی بود
خواهش تحریر نامه بنام هر یک از شما فرمود   انجام در عهدهٔ او بود
دنا کرد   و از تخلف بنجات یافت   و لمس تر مسارم زیرا
ندارم   و نتوانم که با این نفراد نامه نگارم   المجبور معذور در و معاف
العفو   یک نامه نگاشتم   دید که یاران روحانی بر دلم شکل الواح
یک بر برید   و انوار یک شمس   و اوراد یک حدیقه   و شیران یک بیت
معینه   و مرغان یک چمن   در یاین یک گلشن   لهذا حکم یک لگن
دارید   و این نامه فی الحقیقة هر یک مرقوم   انگر فضل و عنایت جمال ابهی
نمایید که چنین شی و حدت نوزان بر افروخت   و عالم انسانی روشن
سند   در اتحاد   و اتفاق اگر خللی از قصور خود هاست   و الا فضل ابهی
کل را دنیل یک جمیع جح فرمود   و نظر جباست ابدیه دمید و نفخه
و حدت عالم انسانی بنام مسجد   حال شما نب و دور جهان گیر
نمایید   مطالع انوار توحید گردید   و مشرق انوار تجرد شوید   تا یاد گار
بنمایید محبت جهان آمیز شش با بید که سحاب الطاف فیضان بر آمد
و انوار گشایش بتابید   من در لیل و نهار و شام و اسحار تضرع نمایم
اسرار نمایم   و از برای شما ثبوت و قرار و راست و یقین بخت در ین
مشئون از حضرت پروردگار طلبم   و علیکم البهاء الابهی

ع ع

Translation appears on p. 41

همواره

ای جوان ربانی همواره در خاطر بودی و بیاد است و الوفیم ایام
ملاقات فراموش نگشته روی و خوبت همواره در نظر است د
از ملکوت آبا است نا بدایت ظیم که روز بروز نخوشتر و بشیر بیاز
گردی بجلا و ث بحبت الله کام و نثیرین نمائی و سبب نوست
استغنا است یاران نازنین گردی نا نجرۀ حیات حیات کرمی بخشد ور
عبدالبهاء ارزی نماید و علیک البهاء الابهی ع ع

Translation appears on p. 42

Translation appears on p. 43

Translation appears on p. 44

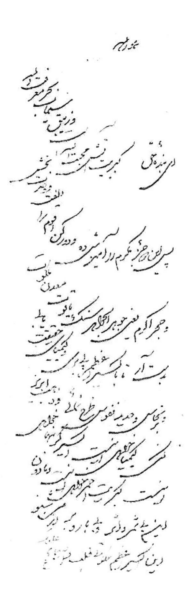

Translation appears on p. 45

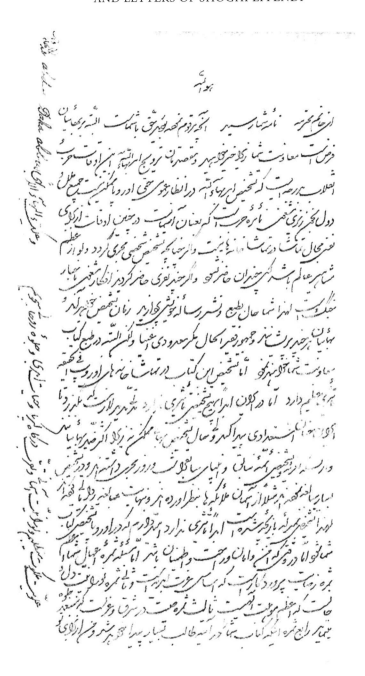

Translation appears on pp. 46–47

هو الله

Translation appears on pp. 48–49

Translation appears on pp. 50–51

Translation appears on pp. 52–53

94

Translation appears on p. 54

Translation appears on pp. 55–56

96

Translation appears on pp. 55–56

Translation appears on pp. 59–60

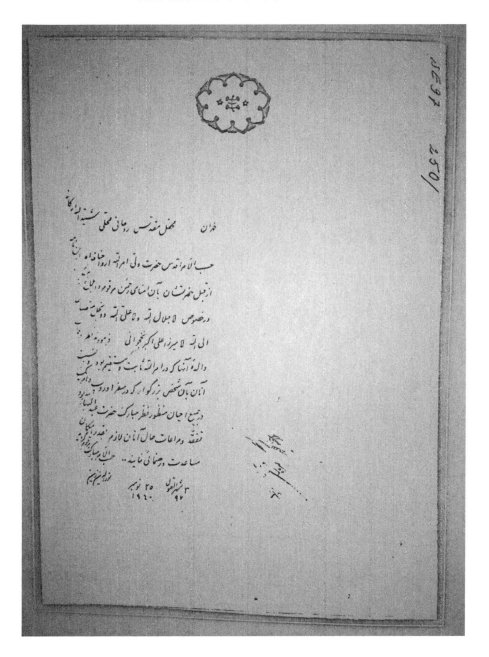

Translation appears on p. 61

Appendix I

Biographical Notes

Parenthetical references refer to the numbered translations of Tablets and letters addressed to Mírzá ʿAlí-Akbar-i-Nakhjavání and other believers in Bákú found on pages 21–66.

ʿAbdu'l-Kháliq presumed to be Mírzá ʿAbdu'l-Kháliq-i-Yaʿqúb-Zádih, an early believer of Bákú, who had been taught the Faith by Mullá Sádiq the Martyr. According to the digest of information from Ishráq-Khávarí's epitome of the history of the Baháʾí Faith in Bákú, he kept a shop in the city and was esteemed as a learned exponent of the Cause; while in Niʿmatuʾlláh-i-Dhaká'íy-i-Baydá'í's "Tadhkiriy-i-Shuʿaráy-i-Qarn-i-Avval-i-Baháʾí" ("Memorials of the Poets of the First Baháʾí Century"), he is recorded to have been an able poet, who went under the pen-name of "Yúsif" or "Yúsif-i-Qafqází" (i. e. "Joseph [the Caucasian]"). (Item 17)

Abu'l-Faḍl, Mírzá the "learned" and "illustrious" Baháʾí author who wrote in Arabic and Persian a number of apologetic works about the Cause, including "The Behai Proofs (Hujajul Beheyyeh)." (Item 14)

Abu'l-Hasan-i-Ardikání, Ḥájí surnamed "Amín-i-Iláhí" ("Divine Trustee"), but better known among the friends as "Ḥájí Amín," the second Trustee of Ḥuqúqu'lláh, following Ḥájí Sháh-Muḥammad-i-Manshádí, surnamed "Amínu'l-Bayán" ("Trustee of the Bayán").

Afnán, Áqá Mírzá Muhsin husband of ʿAbdu'l-Bahá's second daughter Túbá Khánum. (Item 12)

Ahmadov thought to be, possibly, one of the Ahmadov brothers, sons of Ḥájí Aḥmad-i-Mílání, who were resident in Tbilisi, the capital of Georgia. (Item 12)

'Alí-Akbar, Shaykh presumed to be the martyr Shaykh 'Alí-Akbar-i-Qúchání, who, in 1327 A.H. (1909 A.D.), was directed by the Master to take up residence in Bákú in order to nurture its burgeoning Bahá'í community. (Items 15, 4, 7, 13)

Atrpet, Sargis Mubagajian (1860–1937), referred to in these letters as an "Armenian (gentleman / person)," who composed two works having a significant bearing on the Bábí and Bahá'í Faiths: the first, published in Armenian in 1906 (Russian translation 1909), was titled "Imamat: Strana Poklonnikov Imamov" ("Imámate: The Country of the Worshippers of the Imám"); and the second, published in Russian in 1910, was titled "Babizm i Bekhaizm" ("Bábism and Bahá'ism"). (Items 2, 3, 7, 16)

Baghdádí, Ḍíyá'u'lláh youngest son of Áqá Muḥammad-Mustafá, a notable Bahá'í author, who for a number of years edited the Persian section of *Star of the West*. A resident of Chicago, he was known among the Western friends as "Doctor Zia (Ḍíyá')." (Item 27)

Bálá, Ustád Áqá a local believer and champion of the Cause, who, together with his brother Ustád 'Alí-Ashraf, constructed the first purpose-built meeting-place for the friends in Bákú; in view of the brothers' subsequent efforts in rearing the original structure of the Shrine of the Báb, two of its doors were named in their honor—the Báb-i-Bálá and the Báb-i-Ashraf. (Item 7)

Browne, Edward Granville of Pembroke College, Cambridge, who composed the only pen portrait of the Founder of the Faith by a Western author. (Item 8)

Dreyfus-Barney, Hippolyte the first French Bahá'í, designated by the Guardian as one of the nineteen Disciples of 'Abdu'l-Bahá. (Item 14)

Fáṭimih Khánum wife of Mírzá 'Alí-Akbar-i-Nakhjavání. (Items 25, 27)

Grinevskaya, Isabella a Russian Jewish authoress who became a believer in the Cause, and composed various literary pieces on the subject. (Items 5, 6, 7, 8, 9, 14, 23, 24)

Gülnár the Russian countess and authoress Olga Sergeyevna Lebedeva, a contemporary of Tolstoy, whose pen name was at first "Madame Gülnar," then simply "Gülnar." She attracted the favorable notice of Ahmed Midhat, an Ottoman literary figure of the Tanzimat period, who, from 1878, published the newspaper Tercüman-ı Hakikat ("Interpreter of Truth"). Ahmed Midhat Efendi, as he was called, is to be distinguished from Ahmed Midhat Pasha, an eminent Ottoman statesman, and leader of the 1876 constitutional movement, who, as Governor of Syria (1878–81), invited 'Abdu'l-Bahá to visit Beirut (an event commemorated in Bahá'u'lláh's Tablet of the Land of Bá'), and is counted by the Guardian among "those men of eminence and learning who were moved, at various stages of 'Abdu'l-Bahá's ministry, to pay tribute not only to 'Abdu'l-Bahá Himself but also to the Faith of Bahá'u'lláh."—*God Passes By*, p. 316 (Items 6, 7)

Haydar-'Alí, Ḥájí Mírzá "outstanding Persian Bahá'í teacher and author. He spent nine years in prison and exile in Khartúm, traveled extensively in Írán, and passed away in 1920 in the Holy Land. Western pilgrims knew him as the Angel of Mount Carmel."—*Tablets of Bahá'u'lláh Revealed after the Kitáb-i-Aqdas*, p. 57 (Items 13, 25)

Kíshí, Áqá presumed to be Karbilá'í Áqá Kishíy-i-'Alíov, an early believer of Bákú, who had been taught the Faith by Mullá Sádiq the Martyr (Item 7). Mullá Sádiq the Martyr is to be distinguished from Mullá Sádiq-i-Urdúbádí, a founding figure of the Bahá'í Faith in Russia, who, during the eighteen-forties, in the Nakhchivan region of Azerbaijan, preached the imminent advent of the Promised One of Islám; in which role (following his exile to Warsaw by the Russian authorities on account of the disturbances to which his preaching gave rise), he was succeeded by Siyyid 'Abdu'l-Karím-i-Urdúbádí, who is extolled by Bahá'u'lláh in a Tablet quoted earlier in this document. At the beginning of the foregoing digest of information from Ishráq-Khávarí's epitome of the history of the Bahá'í Faith in Bákú it is stated: "At the time when Siyyid 'Abdu'l-Karím was resident in Bákú, a number of persons became believers in the Cause of the Báb. After his passing, the believers of Bákú were left shepherdless, not knowing where to turn, until Mullá Sádiq the Martyr, who previously, whilst in Qazvin, had embraced the Cause of both the Báb and Bahá'u'lláh, returned to Bákú." As recorded in that same digest, Mullá Sádiq the Martyr was killed by the bullet of an assassin at the home of his sister in the village of Zábrát.

Lisa Khánum wife of Áqá Músá Naqíov. (Items 25, 26)

Naqíov, Áqá Músá an early believer of Bákú who, unexpectedly discovering oil on his property, wished to use his newfound wealth to construct a Mashriqu'l-Adhkár in Bákú. (Items 1, 7, 13, 15, 16, 21, 25, 26)

Tolstoy, Leo the celebrated Russian author and seer. (Items 3, 5, 14, 15)

Zínat Khánum wife of Ḍíyá'u'lláh Baghdádi, and younger sister (by two years) of Fáṭimih Khánum. (Item 27)

Appendix II

Digest of Information from I<u>sh</u>ráq-<u>Kh</u>ávarí's Epitome of the History of the Bahá'í Faith in Bákú

At the time when Siyyid 'Abdu'l-Karím was resident in Bákú, a number of persons became believers in the Cause of the Báb. After his passing, the believers of Bákú were left shepherdless, not knowing where to turn, until Mullá Ṣádiq the Martyr, who previously, whilst in Qazvin, had embraced the Cause of both the Báb and Bahá'u'lláh, returned to Bákú. Even before his arrival, tidings of the Revelation of Bahá'u'lláh had reached that city, and a few persons had recognized His claim, among them 'Abdu'l-Manáf, Mustafá Bik, Áqá Bikov, Zargaruf-i-Buzurg, Áqá Javád-i-Sulaymání, and several other souls—none of whom had a sufficient grasp of the Cause. When Mullá Ṣádiq the Martyr arrived in Bákú, he brought with him a copy of the Kitáb-i-Íqán and many other Tablets and Writings; and since, during his previous three-month sojourn in Qazvin, he had acquired from the Bahá'í teachers a sufficient understanding of the fledgling Faith, his arrival in the Caucasus was a great bounty for the believers.

Mullá Ṣádiq was immediately successful in convincing a number of persons of the truth of the Cause; among them Mullá Abú-Ṭálib-i-Karímov, 'Abdu'l-Mu'min-i-Zargaruf, Mír 'Allám, and Karbilá'í Áqá Ki<u>sh</u>íy-i-'Alíov.[1] In Ganjih, Kúk-<u>Ch</u>áy,[2] Salyán,[3] and Bálá-<u>Kh</u>ánlí (Bálá-<u>Kh</u>ání) too the Faith was proclaimed, and a number of persons embraced it. Once the Faith was established in Bákú, and the friends became sufficiently informed of its nature, regular teaching activities were initiated, and inquirers would visit the homes of the friends in order to find out about the new Cause. In consequence, the <u>Sh</u>í'a 'ulamá began inflicting harm and injury on those who had enlisted under its banner.

When Mír 'Allám embraced the Cause, he made his home a "teaching house" ("*bayt-i-tablí<u>gh</u>*"). Hence, from 1890 onwards the Bákú friends

105

had a meeting-place of their own; and this house became subsequently the Ḥaẓíratu'l-Quds of Bákú. Then, in 1906 the friends set about constructing a purpose-built Ḥaẓíratu'l-Quds—a development which caused an outcry from the local Muslims, who protested that the Bahá'ís were constructing a "mosque," which it was incumbent upon them to destroy.

Ustád 'Alí-Ashraf and Ustád Bálá were two brothers who were in charge of the building operations. The latter, who was something of a "strongman," and quite intrepid, announced that he would kill whoever presumed to destroy the Ḥaẓíratu'l-Quds. Ustád Bálá, who was always present on the building site, had secured the services of a government agent in order to ensure that disorderly members of the populace should not create disturbances. A number of the Bahá'ís of Bálá-Khánlí, and the youth of Bákú, as well as a company of elders, were also continually present in the Ḥaẓíratu'l-Quds, keeping watch against the possibility of trouble. Ustád Ashraf and Ustád Bálá, moreover, in view of the building operations, always had on hand some fifty permanent workers and builders. This workforce too was on its guard lest anyone should attack the building; while Ustád Bálá had a license to bear small arms about his waist.

One day at noon, a group of approximately two hundred persons, comprising mullás, siyyids, business people, porters, workers, thieves, ne'er-do-wells, and others, at the instigation of the mullás poured into Chadrovaya (Mirza Aga Aliyev) Avenue, with the intention of destroying the Ḥaẓíratu'l-Quds. As this host drew on apace, the government agent at first attempted to impede their progress, but was overwhelmed by their sheer number. Those outside the building then took refuge within; whereupon, from atop the building, Ustád Bálá cried out "Have at them!" At this, children from all sides, and workers and builders armed with wooden staves, maces, tiles, spades, and pickaxes, launched upon them a concerted attack. The trouble-makers took to flight, but not before about twenty-five of them had been apprehended, including three mullás, two siyyids, three religious students, and two convicted thieves—the rest of their number being made up of business people, workers, and porters. All these were hauled off to the police station, and subsequently released after recognizances of good conduct had been secured from them. Thereafter no one dared to so much as set foot in the vicinity of the Ḥaẓíratu'l-Quds.

The 'ulamá, however, did not rest quiet, and were forever inciting the people to harm the friends, so that, in venturing into the streets, the friends would often encounter abuse or be pelted with dirt; and they would have difficulty in either making purchases from local vendors, or selling their own goods and wares. On account of this persecution, the houses of the Bahá'ís were for the most part clustered around the Ḥaẓíratu'l-Quds, which was where the Russians, Armenians, and Jews also had their homes.

One day, Ḥájí Qalandar invited Músá Naqíov for lunch, and Ḥájí Qalandar accordingly went to the butcher's to purchase some meat. The Ḥájí happening by chance to touch a side of meat, the butcher brought down a meat cleaver upon his hand so forcibly that he broke one of his fingers; and, uttering several choice invectives against his faith and creed, demanded that he pay the cost of the whole side of meat. Without a word, the Ḥájí paid the full cost, and, returning to the Ḥaẓíratu'l-Quds, went about preparing lunch; nor did he say anything about the incident to the servant of the Ḥaẓíratu'l-Quds, who was a believer, and himself a brave and fearless person.

During lunch, the Ḥájí partook of his fare using only his left hand; upon observing which Músá Naqíov inquired of him why his hand was bandaged. The Ḥájí at first kept silence; but then, at Músá's insistence, recounted the incident; whereupon Músá Naqíov telephoned Ustád Bálá, bidding him come to the Ḥaẓíratu'l-Quds as soon as possible.

What then ensued, Ustád Bálá himself relates as follows:

I at first imagined that some rabble must have attacked the Ḥaẓíratu'l-Quds, and for this reason assembled a party of some ten to fifteen builders and workers, armed with staves, maces, spades, and pickaxes. In company with two of the friends who were always by me, we made our way to the Ḥaẓíratu'l-Quds. Yet on our arrival, there was no one to be seen. "Assuredly," I said to myself, "They are in the courtyard within." Yet here too there was no one to be seen. I then proceeded to the room of Ḥájí Qalandar, and, on finding there Músá, the servant, and the Ḥájí partaking of their lunch, I returned to the builders and workers, and dispatched them about their business. Then, in company with those two believers, I returned to the Ḥájí and Músá, and asked "What has befallen, that you so urgently summoned me? I was much alarmed, fearing lest the Ḥaẓíratu'l-Quds had come under attack." Músá replied, "Yet worse has befallen. The Ḥájí's hand has been broken, and he has been beaten and abused. What more did you want them to do?'"

At this, Ustád Bálá betook himself straightway to the butcher; and, having administered to him a sound beating; cast all the meat in his store out into the street; and, having thrown his premises into utter confusion, he addressed him: "Wretched man! I too am a Bahá'í. Hurl your obloquies at me, if you dare!" A group of people had by this time congregated, and the butcher was delivered from the hands of Ustád Bálá.

No more than some two hundred meter's distance from the Ḥaẓíratu'l-Quds was an important business thoroughfare called Varvarinskaya (Hagigat Rzayeva), in which many butchers and grocers had their premises. The proprietors of these businesses comprised Muslims, Armenians, and Jews, all of whom knew the Bahá'ís, and especially Ustád Bálá. To the same degree that Ustád 'Alí-Ashraf was meek and unassuming, his brother Ustád Bálá was over-bearing and assertive.

His Holiness 'Abdu'l-Bahá, in a Tablet to Ustád Bálá, says: "O Bálá! Thou art called by all 'Bálá' ('Exalted'); yet I for my part call thee 'balá' ('calamity'), inasmuch as thou art a calamity unto the enemies of the Cause of His Holiness the All-Merciful. "

The shopkeepers thus all knew how they should comport themselves towards the Bahá'ís; and who, if they harmed them, they would have to deal with. "As long as I am alive," Ustád Bálá one day reassured the friends, "You need have nothing to fear, since the rules to which I am subject are different from those which apply in your case."

Áqá 'Abbás-Mírzá Úrchov relates the following:

When I was a child of but twelve years, I was returning home one day from school when Mírzá 'Abdu'l-Kháliq, whose shop lay on my way, accosted me with a request to order him some meat broth from a local restaurant owner. I did as he bade me, but, when I relayed to him 'Abdu'l-Kháliq's order, the restaurant owner asked me: "Are you a Bahá'í?" "Yes," I replied "I am a Bahá'í, and the nephew of 'Abdu'l-Kháliq." He straight-away seized me by the collar, and slapped me violently upon the face; and when I fell to the ground, he kicked me several times for good mea-sure, and, turning to the young servitors, said, "Lads, take him behind the shop, and deal with him in such-and-such a fashion!" I immediately took to my heels, with them in hot pursuit; but they were unable to keep pace with me, and finally gave up the chase. On returning to Mírzá

'Abdu'l-Kháliq, and tearfully relating to him what had passed, he merely laughed. "Why are you laughing, Uncle?" I protested. "Because," he replied, "When someone suffers in the way of truth, his faith only grows the stronger. As from today, you are a Bahá'í my dear. Be thankful that you were beaten for your faith, not for any wrongdoing."

At this precise moment Ustád Bálá arrived at the shop of Mírzá 'Abdu'l-Kháliq in order to purchase some cigarettes. On observing my tearful state, he inquired of my uncle what he had done to occasion this. "Nothing at all!" my uncle exclaimed, at the same time signaling to me to say naught to Ustád Bálá. Turning now to me, Ustád Bálá persisted: "Abbás, why are you crying? What has befallen? Has your father beaten you? It is no matter. A father's chastisement is goodly counsel!" I could contain myself no longer, and blurted out to him the whole tale. Ustád Bálá now turned to Mírzá 'Abdu'l-Kháliq, and said: "Let us both escort 'Abbás Mírzá to the premises of this scoundrel. When we arrive there, do you content yourself with watching, nor involve yourself further in the proceedings." We all three accordingly made our way to the restaurant, where Ustád Bálá, stationing himself squarely within, addressed the proprietor as follows: "Pray inform me, sir, what ill treatment you have received from the Bahá'ís? Have they stolen your property? taken liberties with your wife? treated you harshly? What offence could they have committed for you to have beaten this child, and then ordered that he be taken behind the shop to receive further maltreatment?" "Forsooth!" the proprietor retorted, "What need is there for such a fuss! Has the lantern of the Imám-Zádih been smashed to smithereens that you take on so? To thrash a Bábí is no great matter! If I have beaten him too sparingly, let me repair my omission!" The restaurant owner stepped forward to make good his threat, but was prevented by an irate Ustád Bálá, who versed the contents of a pan full of food over his head. People now congregated, and delivered the proprietor and his assistants, who had been scalded and beaten, from the hands of Ustád Bálá. Meanwhile the police arrived, and bore off all present on the scene. When, however, Ustád Bálá established their malevolent intention towards the child, they detained the restaurant owner, while releasing his assistants.

Friends, do not imagine that Ustád Bálá confined his ministrations to non-Bahá'ís! On the contrary, if any Bahá'í were guilty of an improper action, Ustád Bálá would correct him too. Ustád Bálá used to say: "My father suffered greatly at the hands of wrongdoers. Now, in the presence of His Holiness 'Abdu'l-Bahá, he is very happy."[4]

Mullá Ṣádiq was successful in convincing a number of people of the truth of the Cause; among them Mullá Abú-Ṭálib-i-Karímov, Mírzá 'Abdu'l-Kháliq-i-Ya'qúb-Zádih, Mír 'Allám, Karbilá'í Áqá Kishí, 'Abdu'l-Mu'min-i-Zar-Gráf, and Mashhadí Ghulám-Ḥusayn. From Bákú he proceeded to Salyán, teaching the Faith in that city to Áqá Javád-'Alíy-i-Yúsif and Mashhadí Shukr(u'lláh)-i-Faraj-Zádih, and in the city of Lankarán to Mullá Áqá and Mashhadí Khayru'lláh. Returning thence to Bákú, he spent a few days at the home of Karbilá'í 'Imrán in Bálá Khánlí, succeeding also in converting his host to the Faith of Bahá'u'lláh. Mullá Ṣádiq was a fearless teacher of the Cause, who acted with an audacity unique to himself, nor shrank from publicly shaming the 'ulamá.

One year, Mullá Ṣádiq went on pilgrimage to the Holy Land, traveling from the port of Bátúm (Batumi) by way of the Black Sea to Istanbul. On his arrival, however, he learned that Bahá'u'lláh had been exiled to 'Akká, and accordingly tarried several months in that city, saving up for the journey by trading in cinnamon tea. He became acquainted with a number of the local friends, and finally departed for 'Akká after a sojourn of a little over three months. Bahá'u'lláh was at that time confined to the military barracks, where He was subject to the harshest restrictions.[5] Discovering, after his arrival, how matters stood, Mullá Ṣádiq sought out the head of the watch, and represented to him: "I am a native of Caucasia, and a Turk, and the provision for my way is now exhausted. Nor have I gainful employment in these parts. Prithee allow me to enter the presence of the venerable Iranian Shaykh who is confined here, in order that I may beseech of him provision for my way, and so return home." The officer of the watch replied: "Come here tomorrow morning when the provisions have been purchased, and I shall send you instead of the porter into His presence." The next day Mullá Ṣádiq, having picked up the provisions, came into the presence of Bahá'u'lláh, and fell before His blessed feet, filled with gratitude that he had attained his heart's desire. Bestowing upon him a lira, Bahá'u'lláh bade him, "Return at once to the Caucasus to teach the Cause. Thou wilt be confirmed and assisted. God is thy helper and supporter."

Mullá Ṣádiq was now no longer the same Mullá Ṣádiq as he had been before: his entire being had been set ablaze with a world-enkindling fire. Returning to Bákú by the same route, he met with the friends in Bátúm, Tiflís (Tbilisi), and

Kúk-_Ch_áy, cheering them with tidings of the Revelation of the Abhá Beauty. After the ascension of Bahá'u'lláh, Mullá Ṣádiq exerted great efforts to ensure that none of the friends would join the violators, exhorting them to remain steadfast in the Covenant.

The Caucasian friends, however, were alarmed by the intrepidity and unwisdom of Mullá Ṣádiq. He had sworn an oath to "shame the mullás," and accordingly would parade himself in the street arrayed in a turban, and grasping in his hand a bottle which, in place of wine, he had filled with water, and from which, ever and anon, he would take an ostentatious swig, pretending the while to be drunk. A number of the friends complained of these antics to His Holiness 'Abdu'l-Bahá, Whose only reply was to preserve silence. In the year 1897, Mullá Ṣádiq addressed a letter to the Master, in which he besought the death of a martyr, receiving in reply a Tablet, from a particular verse of which it was possible to divine that his boon had been granted. On receiving this Tablet, Mullá Ṣádiq arose with the ardor of an impassioned lover. In all the mosques, bazaars, and thoroughfares, he proclaimed boldly the Word of God; and, that he might take leave of the friends, he traveled to all parts, returning after a brief period to Bákú.

Near Bákú lies a village by the name of Zábrát, wherein dwelt Mullá Ṣádiq's sister, to whom he was much attached. Since, at the time of his return from his travels, it was the summer season, he proceeded thither to spend a few days with his beloved sister. This lady, although a believer in the Cause, did not announce the fact, for fear of the reaction of her father and kinsfolk, and as a precaution lest, like her brother, she be deprived of her inheritance. She was at all events a believer, and provided financial assistance to her brother. Her husband too was sympathetic to the Cause, as were the couple's children.

One day at six o'clock in the morning, Mullá Ṣádiq was occupied with his matutinal devotions when he was struck in the forehead by a bullet, surrendering his spirit on the spot. His sister reported the fatality to the Bahá'ís of Bákú; and, since the inhabitants of the village would not consent to his being buried in the local cemetery, they interred him in his sister's garden. Three years later, this lady too passed away, and since she had willed that, in the event of her dying in Zábrát, she should be buried next to her brother, her husband and family laid her to rest in that same spot. When the news of the martyrdom of Mullá Ṣádiq reached 'Abdu'l-Bahá, He revealed for him an ode and a visitation Tablet, the text of which may be inspected in the volume *Muhádirát*.[6]

One of those to whom Mullá Ṣádiq had introduced the Faith was Mír 'Allám, who was a notable figure in those parts. He came from a family of well-to-do Muslims, who were prominent among the Shí'ihs. Mír 'Allám owned a large old building in the heart of Bákú, with nigh on fifty chambers, all of which were let out to Russian, Armenian, and Jewish tenants. Since the building was located in a part of the city favored by Europeans, Mír 'Allám and his wife found themselves the only Muslims in their neighborhood. The couple had no children; and, when Mír 'Allám became a believer, he donated his house to the Cause. At first, he placed several chambers at the disposal of the friends for use as a "teaching house" ("*bayt-i-tablígh*"); but in 1896 he evicted several tenants, converting the premises into a large salon in which gatherings could be held. Again in 1900, he evicted another fifteen tenants, preserving only six of the original chambers, and demolishing the remainder to make room for a central courtyard.

In the near vicinity of Bákú was another village called Bálá-Khánlí. Here there lived a person by the name of Mashhadí Amír, who was by profession an assassin: that is, his services might be hired to dispatch whoever his hirer wished to dispose of. One day Mashhadí Amír went to a Mullá—'Abdu'lláh by name, an Iranian—and addressed him thus: "Master, I have in my life slain many people, and am a sinner. What can I do that God may forgive me?" The Mullá answered him, "If you perform the following three tasks, God will forgive you, and assign to you an exalted chamber in Paradise." "What, pray, are they," Mashhadí Amír eagerly inquired. "First," Mullá 'Abdu'lláh replied, "You must purchase a gilt-embossed and gold-illuminated Qur'án, and give it to me. Each day I read it, the reward thereof will be yours. Second, you must for a period of ten days during the month of Muharram expend your substance upon the poor. Third, you must slay a Bahá'í. Then will your sins be wholly atoned for, and God will forgive you."

Mashhadí Amír first purchased the Qur'án, and bestowed it upon the Mullá. Twenty days later, when the month of Muharram arrived, for a period of ten full days he expended his substance upon the poor. On the fifteenth day of Muharram, he fell to thinking "Whose death can I compass, from which I shall derive the greatest recompense?" After revolving the matter in his mind at length, he eventually resolved to betake himself to Bákú, and there to slay Mír 'Allám, who was reputed as the head of the Bahá'ís. On the sixteenth day of the month of Muharram, therefore, he journeyed to that city, arriving before the Ḥazíratu'l-Quds, which is where the house of Mír 'Allám was situated. On spying him there, Mír 'Allám gave him a hearty greeting, saying, "My good Mashhadí Amír! How fortuitous that you should have remembered us! Do give us the honor of stepping inside, so that we may converse awhile." Mashhadí Amír thought to himself "With what wondrous ease he has fallen into my grasp! I can dispatch him now, and make good my escape! The coast is clear, so no one will detain me." Yet before he could realize his nefarious design, Mír 'Allám took him by the hand, sat him down beside him, and began to speak with him. "My dear," he counselled him, "Almighty God—exalted be He—has created us for the sake of obedience, and to serve his creatures. We must obey the Messengers, Vicegerents, and Imáms, not the enemy of mankind." For well-nigh two hours Mír 'Allám addressed him in this vein, and shortly before noon, he invited him for lunch, to which Mashhadí Amír assented, saying to himself "This is even better! I shall kill him in his own home, and no one will ever see me!" Yet when lunch was over, Mír 'Allám resumed his counsels; and eventually, at about seven o'clock, Mashhadí Amír became completely transformed, and accepted the Cause.

That evening he spent at Mír 'Allám's residence in Bákú. The next morning, having partaken of morning tea, he made his way to Bálá-Khánlí, arriving at midday outside the mosque. Dragging Mullá 'Abdu'lláh down from the pulpit, he seized from him the Qur'án he had given him, admonishing him as follows: "Did you not tell me—godless miscreant that you are!—that the Bahá'ís have 'no religion,' and are used to revile the Prophet, the Qur'án, and the Vicegerents? Well, I have made my own inquiry, and discovered that it is *they* who are the true Muslims, not *you,* who are but a godless miscreant! I have become a Bahá'í, and have nothing further to do with you. May the Lord guide you." Leaving precipitately the mosque, he went to the homes of Karbilá'í 'Imrán and Amír Khalíl, and, much to their delight, announced to them, "I have become a Bahá'í!" After accepting the Faith, Mashhadí Amír became a person of good character, and from that day forth ceased carrying with him a revolver, as had been his wont.

Two months later, one of Mashhadí Amír's enemies fired a bullet at him in the street, and promptly took to flight. Mashhadí Amír, who was injured, had to be taken to the hospital, where he was questioned by the police "Who was it that shot you?" "I know him not," was his reply. Later, he sent a message to his assailant, informing him, "Since I am now a Bahá'í, I did not inform the police of your identity, nor intend to seek vengeance of you." That person subsequently came to Mashhadí Amír to request his pardon, which the latter granted.

His Holiness ʿAbduʾl-Bahá in America told the friends: "Mashhadí Amír, who had been an assassin, having once embraced the Cause became the model of meekness. This is what can happen when one believes wholeheartedly in the True One."

In 1904 Mír ʿAllám abandoned this mortal life.

In 1905 [sic] the friends of Bákú and Caucasia began work on the construction of the Ḥaẓíratuʾl-Quds of Bákú.

In 1907 the aforementioned building was completed.

In 1917 a children's school was constructed beside the Ḥaẓíratuʾl-Quds.

In 1919 an auditorium and theatre were constructed for the youth.

The wife of Mír ʿAllám winged her flight heavenward in 1906.

Mír ʿAllám had Tablets from both the Ancient Beauty and His Holiness ʿAbduʾl-Bahá.

* * *

Mullá Abú-Ṭálib was the son of Mullá Karím, a native of Bákú, who belonged to the clerical class. Abú-Ṭálib was taught the Faith by Mullá Ṣádiq, forswearing thereafter any further connection with mosque and minbar. Abú-Ṭálib became at once notorious among the people for having "turned Bábí," and was subjected to much abuse.

Ustád ʿAlí-Ashraf relates the following:

> Whenever my father had occasion to go abroad into the streets, his whole apparel would always, on his return home, have been soiled and stained: for the shopkeepers were wont to pelt his head and countenance with whatever rotten eggs and decomposed tomatoes they had to hand. When we two brothers were small, we could not protect our father. (Ustád ʿAlí-Ashraf and Ustád Bálá were the sons of Mullá Abú-Ṭálib.) Whenever my father wished to venture forth, my mother would attempt to prevent him, saying, "If you go forth, they will sully your apparel, and subject you to indignity!" But he would always reply, "I must needs go forth and teach the people; and this very injury and maltreatment I receive is in itself a form of proclamation of the Cause."

Abú-Ṭálib was a quiet and mild-mannered person, and a devoted teacher of the Cause. Whatever Tablets he received he would transcribe in his own hand,

and distribute among the friends. His final days were spent in the blessed presence of 'Abdu'l-Bahá in Haifa, in which city he passed away.

Ustád 'Alí-Ashraf, the son of Abú-Ṭálib-i-Karímov, was a native of Bákú, and a Bahá'í by birth. He grew up to be a renowned architect, who undertook the construction of all major state and civic edifices. He was moreover reputed for his probity, and withal comfortably circumstanced from a financial point of view, owning a substantial five-story dwelling situated beside the Ḥaẓíratu'l-Quds of Bákú. When 'Abdu'l-Bahá determined to rear the Shrine of the Báb, He summoned Ustád 'Alí-Ashraf to the Holy Land, and bade him prepare a design for the structure. Dutifully obeying the Master's bidding, he prepared such a design, and presented it to 'Abdu'l-Bahá, Who approved it, with some modification, granting permission for the construction work to commence.[7]

Ustád 'Alí-Ashraf relates the following:

When we started work, His Holiness 'Abdu'l-Baha advised me: "'Alí-Ashraf, you are a native of the Caucasus, where the climate is cool. Since you are not used to a hot climate, you must at all times carry with you a parasol." So saying, He bestowed upon me His own parasol, and took His departure. I soon discovered that whatever instructions I issued to the builders and workers, they were unable to grasp my intention. Becoming at length exasperated, I put aside the parasol, and set to work myself. Once I had explained to the laborers their duties, they too began to work to good effect. We labored until late in the afternoon (six o'clock), by which time, since the weather was hot, and I had rather over-exerted myself, I was taken poorly. The next day, still unwell, I arrived for work; and when, as I was working, 'Abdu'l-Bahá graced us with His presence, one of the workers informed Him, "Ustád yesterday took ill with sunstroke." "My dear 'Alí-Ashraf," the Master reproached me, "Did I not tell you, the weather being hot, to carry with you a parasol, lest you be taken ill?" "With the greatest deference," I replied, "how, if I had carried with me a parasol, should I have performed the work you wish to be done? Do you bid the weather of these parts deal clemently with the servants of the Blessed Beauty! Should you choose not to do so, I shall myself visit the Blessed Sanctuary, and, laying hold upon the hem of the Blessed Beauty, entreat Him in this wise!" Smiling, His Holiness 'Abdu'l-Bahá replied, "My dear Ashraf! Would you have me enter into conflict with nature itself!" At all events, from that day onwards I experienced no recurrence of my sickness, and labored each day unremittingly until the work was finished.

One day I went to 'Akká, where the Master instructed me, "My dear Ashraf, one of the Arabs here has a garden, which he is prepared to sell at a very low price. If you have sufficient means, do you purchase it?" I at once obeyed. 'Abdu'l-Bahá said, "Now it has become the Ashraf Garden"—by which name indeed it was subsequently known.

Another day, as we were engaged in rearing the Most Exalted Shrine, a number of inspectors arrived at the building site, and asked me "What are you building here?" "Four rooms and a water cistern," I replied. "We have been informed," they continued, "that 'Abbás Effendi is rearing here a fortress." "With the greatest respect," I assured them, "'Abbás Effendi is a man of peace, not of war. These four rooms do not in any case constitute a fortress; and furthermore these builders and workers, who are all Ottoman subjects, know that we are constructing four rooms." They asked after my home country, which I informed them was the Caucasus. "Are you a Bahá'í," one of them then asked, to which I replied "Indeed I am." The next day, when His Holiness 'Abdu'l-Bahá came to visit the site, He exclaimed "Áfarín, Jináb-i-Ashraf, marhabá, marhabá!"[8]

Once the original masonry structure of the Shrine of the Báb had been completed, His Holiness 'Abdu'l-Bahá named one of its doors after Ashraf, and the other after Bálá—the "Báb-i-Ashraf" and the "Báb-i-Bálá."[9]

Ustád 'Alí-Ashraf had in all eight children: five sons, named Áqá Habíb, Áqá 'Azíz, Áqá 'Ináyat, Áqá Husayn, and Áqá Ismá'íl; and three daughters, named Farangís, Thurayyá, and Mihrangíz. All his children were educated, and firm and steadfast believers.

Ustád 'Alí-Ashraf passed away in 1933 in Bákú, at which time his Holiness the Guardian of the Cause of God lavished upon him many loving expressions of appreciation.

Ustád Bálá, the son of Mullá Abú-Tálib-i-Karímov, was, like his brother, a native of Bákú, a Bahá'í by birth, and an architect by profession. Ustád Bálá was a brave and spirited man, who, from the age of twenty, devoted himself to the service of the Cause, distinguishing himself in particular for the strenuous efforts he exerted in connection with the construction of the Hazíratu'l-Quds of Bákú.

Since the Muslims would not consent that a Ḥazíratu'l-Quds should be built in Bákú, and were determined actively to oppose any move in this direction, when once, despite their opposition, work began on the edifice, Ustád Bálá, together with a number of the youth of Bákú and Bálá-Khánlí, kept watch night and day over the construction, more than once joining battle with parties of assailants, and scattering them in disarray. Ustád Bálá was on every hand the protector of the friends. Unlike his father and brother, he was no meek victim of oppression; and, so far from receiving beatings at the hands of adversaries, was apt rather to administer them himself. He enjoyed respect in government circles, and was moreover a munificent benefactor. "In every age," he would affirm, "someone must needs play the part of a strongman: in the age of His Holiness Muḥammad it was 'Umar Ibn Khattáb; in the age of His Holiness the Báb it was Mullá Ḥusayn of Bushrúyih; and in the age of 'Abdu'l-Bahá it is Bálá Karímov!" Ustád Bálá was honored to come into the presence of His Holiness 'Abdu'l-Bahá, and to receive from Him several Tablets. The Master, Who termed Bálá a "*bálá*" ("calamity") . . . unto the enemies . . . ,"[10] named after him one of the doors of the Shrine of the Báb. Were one to devote a whole volume to the bravery of this man, it would fail to do him justice. He exerted extraordinary efforts to protect the Cause of God and the friends, most especially the youth. He served at all times as a member of the Spiritual Assembly.

Following the Revolution in Caucasia,[11] the minority peoples were enfranchised, and in consequence such classifications as Bábí, Bahá'í, and Jew lost their significance, and no one any longer ventured to lay a finger upon another. Mullá, Ákhund, Siyyid, bravo, assassin—all such categories of persons effectively ceased to exist, and people no longer carried about them revolvers, pistols, and knives. The ruffians too had all been put away by the government.

Ustád Bálá, at the time of the Czarist government, had a license to bear firearms, as a protection both for his own life and property, and for those of the friends. Once the friends were at ease in their minds on this score, they felt they had no further need for Bálá. Thus it was that a number of short-sighted and self-seeking individuals put it about among the friends that Bálá should no longer be elected to the Spiritual Assembly, representing him as an overbearing person, of unregenerate character, inclined to abusive language, and so on and so forth. The Spiritual Assembly accordingly requested the friends to forbear electing him.

During the Riḍván Festival of the year 1918, the friends were assembled in the Ḥaẓíratu'l-Quds for the election, and, having for the most part cast their votes, were waiting for the vote-telling to commence. At this juncture, a courier arrived, bearing two telegrams from the sacred presence of the Master. The friends gathered in the large meeting-room to hear the contents of the telegrams, which were as follows:

First telegram: "I am praying at the Sacred Threshold for your success. 'Abdu'l-Bahá."

Second telegram: "Ustád Bálá, son of Abú-Ṭálib-i-Karímov, is, on the part of 'Abdu'l-Bahá, the permanent member of the Spiritual Assembly of Bákú. Do you elect your own nine members.[12] 'Abdu'l-Bahá 'Abbás"

When this latter telegram was read out, all were abashed, realizing what a great blunder they had committed. A few of the friends suggested "Let us renew the election." Ustád Bálá however instructed: "Open the ballot box, and call out the votes." This being done, it was discovered that Ustád Bálá had received not even a single vote.

Twenty days later, Ustád Bálá arrived in the Holy Land, and, throwing himself at the feet of 'Abdu'l-Bahá, thus adjured Him: "Beloved Master, pray relieve me of membership of the Spiritual Assembly! Assuredly it was because the friends were displeased with me that they chose not to elect me. His Holiness Bahá'u'lláh says that His pleasure is in the pleasure of His creatures.[13] It is therefore up to me to show forth a goodly character in order that the friends may be well pleased with me."

Ustád Bálá subsequently told the friends: "His Holiness 'Abdu'l-Bahá had placed about my neck a chain, which, when I went to visit Him, I succeeded in unloosing.[14] By sending that blessed cable He in reality insured my protection."[15]

Ustád Bálá was twice honored to come into the presence of the Master. He had but one daughter, who married a man named Hajinski, a member of the Czarist parliament.[16] In 1920, when the Soviet army entered Bákú, he was executed by firing squad, his wife passing away two years later. Hajinski had one son, who in 1922 escaped to Iran; in 1941, however, the Russian army, having captured him in Iran, bore him off to Russia, and executed him too by firing squad. Neither Hajinski nor his son were believers in the Cause. Bálá's own wife passed away in 1925; while he himself in 1923 suffered a partial stroke, remaining thereafter permanently confined to his bed.

In the year 1925, a cheque for twenty-five pounds arrived at the household, sent by Ḍíyá'u'lláh Aṣghar-Zádih in London. This was a gift from the Guardian. Upon receiving this donation, he at first wept; but then laughed. Asadu'lláh Zargaruf, the chairman of the Spiritual Assembly, who was present on the occasion, asked him, "Dear uncle [for he was wed to the daughter of Ustád 'Alí-Ashraf], why was it that you at first wept, and then laughed?" He replied, "Asadu'lláh! I wept to think that, during the ministry of his Holiness the Guardian of the Cause of God, I had performed no service; but then I laughed to think what a compassionate master I had, who had not forgotten Bálá, but been mindful of him at the time of his incapacity and sickness."

Ustád Bálá Karímov passed away in the year 1927. All the friends of Bákú, Bálá-Khánlí, Bíbí-Haybat, the Naqíov works, Chúqúr-Yúrd, and Naft-Álán, together with representatives of the Assemblies of Ganjih, Kúk-Cháy, Salyán, and Barda', participated in his funeral obsequies. For no less than three days, the friends held memorial gatherings for him in the Ḥaẓíratu'l-Quds.

* * *

Músá Naqíov was a native of Bákú, who had been born in the village of Baljarí. He was a corn-chandler by profession, and had been taught the Faith by the aforementioned Mullá Ṣádiq.

Ustád 'Alí-Ashraf-i-Karímov relates the following:

Jináb-i-Músá had a business in Baljarí selling provender, and was possessed also of some landed property. When, in the outlying districts of Bákú—Bálá-Khánlí, Baljarí, Naft-Álán, Chúqúr-Yúrd, and Sábún-Chí—oil was discovered, the people, instead of tilling their land, dug in it wells, from which they extracted oil. (In those days, an oil well was excavated like an ordinary well, the oil being extracted from it with a bucket.)

One day, a number of wealthy Muslims approached Músá with an offer to buy from him his land, which he refused. "If you do not wish to sell the land," they persisted, "come let us enter into a joint venture, in which we provide the money, and you the land: then, whatever oil is extracted, half the proceeds shall belong to us, and half to you." To this Músá assented;

and once the arrangement had been formalized in a deed of contract, the work of prospecting began. Over a period of nigh on two years, twenty wells were excavated; yet all of these wells struck either water or the living rock. By this stage, some four thousand manáts had been expended, and with no tangible result.

One day, his partners, in the extremity of their frustration and annoyance, laid violent hands on Músá, and soundly beat him, expostulating, "You such-and-such Bábí turncoat! Since your intention is evil, and your faith untrue, God is wrath with us too for having entered into partnership with a godless miscreant such as yourself! Either you return to us our money, or we shall slay you!" Músá agreed to leave his land in pledge with them for a period of two years, at the end of which, if they had not received their money, the land would be theirs, and a deed was drawn up to this effect.

Músá, in company with one of the friends, proceeded to the land, and instructed the well-digger to cease his operations. The latter however replied, "Áqá Músá! I have labored two whole years in this place, and it is I who have used up all the money, yet without oil having been struck. I pray you, give me leave to dig just one more well: then, if oil be found, do you pay me my wages; but otherwise, if oil be not found, do you pay me naught, and I will render you a deed attesting that I have received my wages."

Músá accepted his offer, and traveled to Bákú in order to draw up a legal instrument formalizing the arrangement. This done, he proceeded straightaway to Ḥájí Qalandar in the Ḥaẓíratu'l-Quds, and related to him the whole proceeding. Ḥájí Abu'l-Ḥasan[17] happened also to be present, so Músá composed a letter, which he handed to Ḥájí Amín,[18] requesting him to convey it to the blessed presence of 'Abdu'l-Bahá. Ḥájí Qalandar wrote a letter of his own, requesting Ḥájí Amín to lay hold upon the hem of His garment, and implore Him to grant a boon with respect to Músá, who was in dire straits. Ḥájí Amín duly attained the presence of 'Abdu'l-Bahá; presented to Him the petitions; and, laying hold upon the hem of His blessed garment, besought Him to bestow a boon upon Músá; to which 'Abdu'l-Bahá replied: "Send a cable to Ḥájí Qalandar saying 'I shall pray for him in the Blessed Sanctuary.[19] God willing, he shall be prospered.'" Immediately the telegram arrived in Bákú, Ḥájí Qalandar sent to Músá the message, "The telegraph has arrived; do you come to the city, for I am occupied here with work."

Músá came to Bákú; and that very afternoon the well-digger brought word that the well he had been excavating had struck oil, which was now gushing forth in a fountain.

Músá was now no longer the same Músá he had been but a few days previously, for, from having been in straitened circumstances, he had become a millionaire! Even before the expiry of the stipulated term, he returned to his partners their investment, saying: "Evidently, then, my faith was true, and my heart pure, that God bestowed oil upon me! Nay, it is your heart and intention that were impure, that He did not so favor you!" Becoming, in the wake of this discovery, a man of substance, Músá now invested in a mechanical derrick; and, returning again to those wells which previously had reached only water and the bedrock, and employing this equipment to sink them deeper, he was successful in striking oil in each case there too. It was not long ere Músá had become a wealthy magnate of the very first order throughout the whole of Russia. Finally, he owned more than one hundred and fifty four- and five-story edifices.

Músá Naqíov had but one son and one daughter. After the death of his first wife (the mother of his children), he took to wife a Russian lady. Then, in 1910 his only son Ismá'íl passed away, and in his name he reared a grand edifice—the Ismá'ílíyyah (Ismailiyye)— bequeathing it to a Muslim benevolent society.[20] Músá's daughter married the son of Shamsí Asadu'lláh, who was a wealthy Muslim.[21] In 1918, during the Armenian-Azerbaijani War,[22] the Armenians set fire to the Ismá'ílíyyah; but in 1919 Músá restored it. The Ismá'ílíyyah serves currently as a library, which is named after the celebrated poet Sábir.[23]

Outside the city, Músá constructed a hospital. The construction of this building, which was planned to contain 2,500 beds,[24] began in 1913, and continued for four years. Yet because of the Russian Revolution, and the consequent severance of ties with foreign lands, when once the building was complete, it could not be regularly fitted out as a hospital, and thus remained in an unfinished state. In 1925, the Soviet government of Azerbaijan brought the project to completion. The hospital, which bore at first the name of Músá Naqíov, is now called after 'Azíz Bikov, a Caucasian revolutionary.[25]

Músá, in order to learn Russian and Turkish, hired three well-known university professors to act as his tutors. In view of his vast wealth, he was one day taken hostage by the revolutionaries, who released him only after receiving a ransom of 250,000 manáts. For this reason, Músá was always escorted by members of the secret police; while around his residence, too, a detail of secret police kept continuous watch.

When, in 1919, Músá passed away, his whole fortune passed to his daughter; or rather to his millionaire son-in-law. Músá was a sincere believer, true-natured, and withal compassionate. He was above all extremely humble. Unlike other millionaires, he was not a gambler, womanizer, or toper, but pious and god-fearing. In 1913, he and Karbilá'í Áqá Kishíy-i-'Alíov had the bounty of coming into the presence of 'Abdu'l-Bahá. In 1911 Músá had purchased a large plot of land in the best part of Bákú for the purpose of constructing there a Mashriqu'l-Adhkár, and the design for this, which he had commissioned from the ablest architects, he now presented to 'Abdu'l-Bahá. "This is an excellent design," the Master responded, "And one to which I shall affix my signature: yet do you the while forbear constructing it; I shall notify you hereafter when to do so." Directly opposite this land the Armenian community, in 1916, constructed a church; but in 1920, the Soviet state destroyed this edifice with dynamite, and replaced it with an open area. Since the land of the Mashriqu'l-Adhkár had been laid out as a garden, and was surrounded by a wall, one part of it was converted into a public park, and the other part into a children's garden in the name of Naríman Narímanov.[26]

Músá was at all times a member of the Spiritual Assembly, whose meetings he would regularly attend. He bore the costs of a Bahá'í teacher, who was quartered in the Hazíratu'l-Quds, as well as those of the Hazíratu'l-Quds, and other expenses too. He paid each month a sum in charitable assistance, and defrayed any extraordinary costs that arose: yet all this, in comparison to his fortune, was of small account. Whenever Hájí Abu'l-Hasan-i-Amín[27] visited Bákú, Músá would pay him a sum in consideration of the "Málu'lláh" ("Property of God")— that is, the portion of his property belonging as of right to God.[28] Yet Hájí Amín, dissatisfied, would reproach him: "Músá, you should pay more than this!"—to which Músá would reply "Hájí, I have numerous outgoings."

On one occasion, Jináb-i-Amín complained to the Master that Músá was making insufficient payments of the "Málu'lláh"; to which His

Holiness 'Abdu'l-Bahá replied: "Músá himself belongs to us; his fortune, however, does not belong to us."

One day, one of the friends, who lived in a lowly part of the city, invited Músá to attend a feast in his home. When Músá duly turned up at the appointed hour, some of the friends present asked him, "Why have you come here? This place is dangerous for you. You might be taken hostage." "Had I not come," Músá replied, "The heart of this person would have been grieved at me. Bahá'u'lláh would not wish me to be a cause of grief to his heart." The whole of the Caucasus, and most of the wealthy magnates of Russia, knew that Músá was a Bahá'í, for he would always say to whomever he met "I am a Bahá'í."[29]

In the year 1913, all the dignitaries, nobles, and wealthy magnates of Russia were invited to a banquet commemorating the three hundredth anniversary of the Romanov dynasty. Músá too was among those invited. When the time came for the company to lift their glasses to toast the health of Nicholas II, Músá raised a glass, which, instead of wine, was filled with water. When some objected to this action on his part, he replied, "I am a Bahá'í. In our religion the consumption of alcohol is forbidden." All the wealthy magnates were either party members or involved in politics. Músá, however, kept himself aloof from such matters; nor belonged to any of the contemporary clubs, which were dens of gambling, alcohol consumption, and political discourse.

One day, Músá said to Hájí Zaynu'l-'Ábidín [Taqíov],[30] "Hájí! This teacher of yours has shown himself to be a man of parts. What do you say to his conversing with a Bahá'í teacher, while we watch, to see which of them gives the better account of himself?" Taqíov assenting to this proposal, it was decided that on Thursday, at three o'clock, the company would foregather at the home of Taqíov. On Thursday, Músá made his way to the Hazíratu'l-Quds to meet Mírzá 'Alí-Akbar-i-Nakhjavání and Mírzá 'Abdu'l-Kháliq, so that he might proceed in their company to the house of Taqíov. Just as they were mounting a kibitka,[31] Mírzá Ismá'íl-i-Mishkát chanced to arrive, and wished to know whither they were bound. The purpose of the visit having been explained to him, it fell out that Mírzá Mishkát too formed one of the company.

After tea and sweet confections had been served, the conversation began in good earnest. Áqáy-i-Jalíl, the teacher of Taqíov, was first to speak, and addressed himself to Mírzá 'Abdu'l-Kháliq. Mírzá Mishkát, however, observing Jalíl to be a sophistical reasoner, himself took charge of the debate on the Bahá'ís' behalf, with the result that Jalíl was over-powered, and all at once exclaimed, "I do not believe in God, Muḥam-mad, or Jesus, that you should seek to convince me with arguments derived from their Books, all of which I consider to be no better than so much empty verbiage." At this, Mírzá Mishkát, turned to Taqíov, begging leave that he might make of Jalíl first a Muslim, and then a Bahá'í! This being granted, Mishkát proceeded to demonstrate the truth of the Divine Messengers, the Imáms, and Vicegerents, Jalíl remaining all the while incapable of opposing him. While thus discoursing, Mish-kát spoke incidentally too of the teachings of Bahá'u'lláh; and at length, at five o'clock, the meeting came to an end.

Taqíov confided to Músá, "This teacher of yours is a great scholar—assuredly he must be the Bahá'ís' Imám." "The reality of the matter," Músá responded, "is quite simply that Jalíl has not the capacity to con-front a Bahá'í. The person of whom you speak is but a humble vendor of stationery, who tramps the streets and markets, selling paper and ink." This, Taqíov found it impossible to credit; yet a few days later, he espied him in the street, carrying before him a tray on which were laid out quantities of paper and ink. He sent his carriage-driver after him, and the latter conducted him back to the carriage. Having instructed the carriage-driver to take from Mishkát his tray, and place it before him in the kibitka, he bade the latter mount his vehicle, and drove him to his home, where the two spent several hours in converse. When the time arrived for Mishkát to depart, Taqíov presented him with an envelope; and on being questioned by his guest as to its contents, he replied, "It contains a sum of money, which, however unworthy it be in respect of your deserts, I request you to use to acquire for yourself a shop premises." To this, however, Mishkát replied, "I am most grateful and thankful for your generous offer; yet I cannot accept your gift, for I have rendered you no service worthy of remuneration. My circumstances, moreover, do not permit me to open a shop, for I must be ever traveling from place to place, occupied with exalting the Word of God, and my present income is quite sufficient to this purpose." However much Taqíov insisted that he accept the gift, he steadfastly refused to do so. As a result of this encounter, Taqíov enfranchised the Bahá'ís employed in his works, becoming himself sympathetic toward the Cause, and granting Mishkát permission to visit his home whenever he might wish to do so.

As mentioned, Músá passed away in 1919, and, in a ceremony of great dignity, his corpse was laid to rest according to the Bahá'í rites. His grave is situated next to that of Ḥájí Qalandar. His whole fortune passed to his daughter and son-in-law. The passing of Músá resulted in the proclamation of the Cause of God throughout the Caucasus.

It was previously stated that Músá, after becoming rich, hired three eminent individuals to act as his tutors. These were: 1) Sulṭán Majíd Ḥamíd Bikov; 2) Ḥasan Bik Áqá Bikov; and 3) Áqá Ḥamíd Jihángír Bikov. Ḥamíd Bikov was the Minister of Culture in the Musavat government,[32] while Áqá Bikov was the Minister of the Interior. Ḥamíd Bikov was in addition a member of the National Assembly of Azerbaijan. These three individuals, after the passing of Músá, claimed that, according to the provisions of Bahá'í Law, they were entitled, as his teachers, to claim a part of his inheritance. A certain number of nephews and nieces also made their appearance at this time. His wife, a Russian, had become a Bahá'í, and obtained from the Spiritual Assembly a formal declaration that Músá had been a Bahá'í; had been interred according to the Bahá'í rites; had provided regular financial assistance to the Cause; had, in the year 1912 [sic], had the honor of visiting 'Abdu'l-Bahá; and had received from the latter a number of Tablets—all of which circumstances she published in the newspaper, presenting at the same time a petition of the like tenor to the Ministry of Justice. Engaging the services of a number of first-rate lawyers, she entered into litigation with Músá's son-in-law; and, after a few sessions, the court ruled that the properties and wealth of the deceased should be distributed according to the provisions of Bahá'í Law. The lawyers set to work on the matter; but at this point legal proceedings were overtaken by events, for, a mere five days ere the destined distribution of the estate, the Bolshevik army of the Soviet State arrived in Bákú. The slate was now wiped clean; and, just as His Holiness 'Abdu'l-Bahá had asserted "Músá himself belongs to us; his fortune, however, does not belong to us," on the very day the Red Army arrived in Bákú, the son-in-law, daughter, and grandchild of Músá were all shot to death—executed in their own home—after which, this file was closed for good and all.

Happy the lot of Músá, that he did not live to witness these events! He, like other persons of substance, would have been cast into prison. He would have been compelled each day to sweep the streets and to clean out the latrines. He would have had to sleep in a dank underground cellar; and, after ten or twenty days, to be executed by firing squad. Then would he have had no grave, no shroud or burial, no prayer or parting orison! Yet that eminent man was laid to rest with great dignity according to the rites of his faith. Memorial gatherings were held for him both in the Ḥaẓíratu'l-Quds and in the mosque, and more than one thousand bouquets of roses were scattered over his grave.

Appendix III

Russia's Cultural Contribution to the Bahá'í Faith
by Martha L. Root

Mrs. Isabel Grinevskaya, a Russian poet in Leningrad, gave a great impetus to the Bahá'í Movement and to world art in her three celebrated writings, the two dramas, "Báb" and "Bahá'u'lláh," and a narrative called "A Journey in [to?] the Countries of the Sun." The last named is an account of her visit to 'Abdu'l-Bahá in 1911 when He was in Ramleh, Egypt. While the last is in prose it has verses introduced so that we might almost say that the three form a trilogy in poetic form presenting the new universal religion of the oneness of mankind proclaimed by those three heavenly personages, the Báb the Forerunner, Bahá'u'lláh the Revealer of the Word and 'Abdu'l-Bahá the Centre of the Covenant of the Bahá'í Faith.

From the point of view of art the dramas rank high. Russian critics affirm that these works have proclaimed their author a poet of the first order. One of her countrymen, Mr. Wesselitzky, President of the Foreign Press Association of London, said that he read the drama "Báb" on a railway train when he was returning to England from Russia in August, 1905. His own words were: "I was at once attracted by the rare combination of philosophical thought with a great power of expression, beauty, imagery, and harmony of verse. I keenly felt the delight of reading a new, great poem and discovering a new first-rate poet. I should have felt so on broad, general grounds from whatever country the poet came! However, my joy was intensified by the fact that the poem had been written in my own language and that the author was a countrywoman of mine."

This article purports to give a little history of these works, for 'Abdu'l-Bahá Himself praised these dramas. (I do not know that He saw the narrative.) When He held the manuscript of the drama "Bahá'u'lláh" in His hands, He blessed it and prophesied to the author that these two dramas would be played in Ṭihrán!

The drama "Báb" was published in May, 1903, and was played in one of the principal theatres in St. Petersburg in January, 1904. It was this drama that first brought to Count Leo Tolstoy a knowledge of the Baháʾí teachings. He read the book and at once wrote to Mrs. Grinevskaya his appreciation of her great drama and his sympathy with the Baháʾí Movement; the letter was printed in the Russian press and the poet has his letter in her possession now.

I have before me as I write a clipping from the "Herold" of January, 1904: "The play *Báb* appeared in May of last year, 1903, the most inconvenient time for the appearance of a book. Nevertheless the pens of the critics began to move in the journals and magazines in order to compose hymn-songs of praise to the author. Moreover an enlightened Persian society sent her an inspired letter of thanks; and above all, Mrs. Isabel Grinevsky had the spiritual satisfaction that among those who eulogized her drama was the lion of contemporary Russian literature, Leo Tolstoy. The impression was such that it made us think that amidst the statists representing the Persian throngs were real Persians; it seemed as if the scene exhaled the perfume of the roses of Shíráz!"

Mr. Wesselitsky, whom I mentioned earlier in this story, gave a lecture in London in 1907 about this drama and his speech was afterwards published in pamphlets in English and French.[1] I quote two paragraphs:

Amidst the sorrows of disastrous war and those dreadful inner troubles, that book "Báb" was my only happy impression, and it remains since a permanent source of joy and comfort as a manifest proof of the vitality of Russia and its creative genius.

The romantic side of this drama, too, is quite original. The plot is not based on adultery as in French drama and not on seduction as in "Faust," but on renouncement and self-sacrifice. The romantic side of the Báb is closely allied with the metaphysical-ethical side. The drama has so much of the latter that every act may seem to be a sermon and the drama itself a suite of sermons. Yet all that preaching is relieved by genuine enthusiasm, eloquence of the heart and real passion. The conflict in the soul of the hero is not between passion and reason, but between two passions—human love and love divine—the latter being stronger and more ardent than the former. It is that manifestation of the power of the higher aims in the heart of man which is the chief feature of this book and the secret of its irresistible charm.

Celebrating the decade of the first performance of "Báb" in January, 1914, Mrs. Grinevskaya gave a great conference on the drama in one of the most beautiful concert halls of Leningrad. The "St. Petersburg Informations Paper" gives the event a long review praising the author and her reading of selections from the poem and her address. One paragraph particularly I remember: "As a characteristic of the frame of mind of the poetess during the creation of her poem, the following words of her own may serve as an illustration: 'A well-known professor told me that the name of my poem, "Báb" does not sound well to the ears of Russians. I answered that the names of the people who preached the ideals of love, paying for those ideals with their lives, must sound well to all those who have ears to hear. All noble ideals are so few in these days that it would be worthwhile to renew the performance of "Báb" in order to awaken the remembrance of these ideals. We, the people of the West, rise too late, we do not know the East where the sun shines!'"

The play was presented again in the Folk Theatre in Leningrad in April, 1917, after the Russian Revolution. People came even from Moscow and Turkistán to see it. Diplomats from foreign countries were in the audience; the ambassador from China was one. A second edition of the drama had been published in 1916, and these books were sold at the entrance of the theatre; many spectators sat with the open books in their hands during this performance. It is a long drama in five acts, equal in the number of verses to "Don Carlos" of Schiller and "Cromwell" of Victor Hugo.

When I wrote asking Mrs. Grinevskaya about these dramas she sent me several letters. I should state that she has written many works along different lines of thought and lectured on many subjects in Russia, and had often spoken in conferences on these two dramas, "Báb" and "Bahá'u'lláh." She was a member of the former Philosophic Society of the University, an active member of the former Oriental Society, and is a member of the present Bibliological Society and several literary societies and unions. She said that before she wrote her poem "Báb," the Russian public generally had not heard much about the Bahá'í Movement. She herself knew about it only from reading. The critics thought she had traveled much in Írán, she was so well informed about the life there, but as a matter of fact she had not been in Írán. She had heard that some Bahá'í believers from Írán had been driven out of their land into Turkey and India, and that some had come to Turkistán and were residing in the cities of Táshkand, 'Ishqábád and Mary and in the city of Bákú in the Caucasus.

"Still, I thought," she says, "these believers in the Báb now called Bahá'ís had mingled with other nations, and perhaps had ceased to exist as a religious entity. The description of Professor Edward G. Browne seemed to me a fairy tale. How astonished I was when, after my drama 'Báb' made its appearance in 1903, I received one day a letter with the following address: 'To the Author of the book "Báb," Mrs. Isabel Grinevskaya in St. Petersburg.' Neither street nor number of the house was marked, yet thanks to the careful postal authorities, that letter, though unregistered, reached me safely."

Both the handwriting and signature proved unknown but she relates: "That letter was from 'Alí-Akbar Mamedhanly from Bákú[2] who wrote that he was a believer in the Báb, that he had read in the *News* of Bákú about my poem, the account of which had interested him greatly and that he would like to get the book. He asked that if he found any mistakes against the Teachings of the Báb, could he perhaps point them out? It was like a star falling from heaven at my feet! As if I had found a precious stone where I had not expected to find one."

The book was mailed to him at once and she explained to that Bahá'í that she had had to deviate just a little from a few of the historical facts for the sake of a dramatic whole. She added: "I wrote for a public all unprepared to hear moral, religious and philosophical ideas from the stage; it was accustomed to lighter plays, not a theme about God, of religion, especially about the conception of a new religion or rather, I would say religion renewed!"

The Bahá'í from Bákú politely replied to Mrs. Grinevskaya's letter as follows: "The impression which I received in reading your drama was such that I could not see any mistakes of any kind, even though I read it many times. We read it in the Bahá'í Assembly (meeting) and the believers send you sincerest thanks. They feel sure that the literary world will soon unite in a general solemnizing of your creative powers."

She said that he also wrote beautifully about the Bahá'í life in Caucasus, stating among other points: "We live here cherishing the tenets for which our grandfathers, fathers and brothers shed their blood maintaining the chief principles: pardon, patience and love to mankind." Mrs. Grinevskaya said that these letters were written in Russian and showed that the Bahá'ís were very enlightened in literature and science. She also added: "It was such a joy to me to find that there are in the world people so congenial to me in feeling and in vision. I loved with my soul those spiritual people who, just like the people in my drama, were holding those principles of pardon, patience and love to all mankind, holding them not as a dead dogma but as a living truth!"

Now I shall speak of the tragedy-poem "Bahá'u'lláh." Mrs. Grinevskaya wrote me how she received the inspiration to write it. She said: "Among the many letters which I received from unknown people, all writing me about my play, 'Báb,' was one from a gentleman who to my astonishment had a profound knowledge not only of the Báb but also of Bahá'u'lláh. Like the Báb, until 1903, Bahá'u'lláh was generally unknown even among the cultured classes, professors sometimes asking me who my hero was. Even one (Czarist) politician had once asked me, 'What is Bahá'u'lláh?' Not who, mind you, but what! So I was all the more impressed to hear from my Russian provincial correspondent the name of Bahá'u'lláh. He said in his note: 'I was fascinated by the poem *Báb* like a youth though I am not a youth in years. I have passed two faculties of the university and have in my library all the available works which appear in the literature of the world.'"

"He counselled me," Mrs. Grinevsky says, "to compose a tragedy about the life of Bahá'u'lláh. I myself had thought of it but had been so occupied I had never attempted it; now I determined to undertake this big work. I always remember with gratitude the memory of this Russian gentleman who was not a Bahá'í but a man of great heart. He passed on before my work was published, and I never met him. His name was Nicolas Zazuline; he, as I knew, was president of the nobility in Kishinef and the author of several philosophical treatises."

She continues: "When my work was finished and notices about it appeared in the press, a number of people who had assisted at the representations of my poem 'Báb,' and had heard my conferences about that poem which I gave many times, asked me to prepare a lecture about my new composition. The first address about it was given in our summer capital Siestroretzk and afterwards I also lectured in the capital itself at the Society of Oratorical Arts' Hall, in the year 1910."

Mrs. Grinevskaya explained that when her Bahá'í correspondent of Bákú, Mírzá 'Alí Akbar Mamedhanly, read in the newspapers that the work was finished (he had known from her that it was being written), he asked to have a copy sent to him. She mailed to him several excerpts from the poem. A few weeks later she was amazed to receive a telegram from him saying: "'Abdu'l-Bahá permits us to visit Him in Egypt." 'Abdu'l-Bahá was at that time making a short stay in Egypt.

She writes in her letter to me: "That had been my secret, my innermost desire, to see with my own eyes those people whom I had described, who, as my correspondent said, 'love all mankind.' I had thought it absolutely impossible, and yet, unexpectedly, wonderfully, it had come to pass that I could go to see even the greatest of those people! I started from Russia with my manuscript of the poem 'Baháʼuʼlláh' in December, 1910, my aim being to see the surroundings of my dreams, of my fancy, about which my former respectful correspondent and present fellow-traveler in that journey to Egypt had spoken—to see ʻAbduʼl-Bahá!"

Seven years had passed between the appearance of the drama "Báb" and the concluding of the tragedy "Baháʼuʼlláh" followed by this memorable journey. Mrs. Grinevskaya spent two weeks in Ramleh, Egypt, as the guest of ʻAbduʼl-Bahá. After she returned to Russia she had several letters or Tablets from Him. In one of these He speaks of an article which He had just received about her poem "Baháʼuʼlláh." From the Tablet (or letter) addressed to Madame Grinevskaya and signed by ʻAbduʼl-Bahá, I quote:

The article which was published in the Saint Petersburg Journal about thy recent book (Baháʼuʼlláh) was in the utmost eloquence and fluency. It was an indication of thy praiseworthy services. The publication of such articles is very useful. They are conducive to the promotion of the divine Call. Praise be to God that thou art assisted in the service of the world of humanity and art spreading the summons of the Kingdom of God. Day and night thou must praise God that thou art assisted to perform such a great service. Rest thou assured that that which is the utmost desire[3] of thy heart shall come to pass concerning this matter.

This seed which thou has sowed shall grow. If the means are not available at present, unquestionably they will become realized. I pray in thy behalf that thou mayest become confirmed in the uninterrupted service of the Kingdom of God.

The article which ʻAbduʼl-Bahá mentions in His Tablet had been published in the French newspaper "Journal de Saint-Petersbourg" January, 1912. The headline was "Baháʼuʼlláh." I quote paragraphs from this review:

Baháʼuʼlláh means the Glory of God—such is the title of the new tragedy with which Mrs. Isabel Grinevskaya has enriched Russian dramatic literature. We must praise without restriction a work whose high, dramatic significance is combined with admirable form. The author of the drama "Báb," that work of such strong thought, has never attained such a powerful conception as this poem.

The mind of the reader, attracted by a rhythm of an unspeakably harmonious poetry, rises imperceptibly to summits where the most grave problems are discussed, problems over which thoughtful humanity bends with fear and despair, helpless to solve them. The characters are analyzed with great psychological insight.

Bahá'u'lláh, the central figure, is depicted with the clearness and power of an antique high-relief. The complexity of that elect-nature is presented with the authority and truth of the great masters of the classical theatre. What a lofty lesson, what eloquence sursum corda in that life of pure bounty, of selflessness in that wide desire to spread peace!

How not to be moved, fascinated by the nobility of this Apostolic character?

As in the "Báb," the events touch the great religious movement which roused the country of Persia in the middle of the last century. The historical part is exact. Mrs. Grinevskaya did not limit herself to the studies of documents, the great quantity of which we can hardly imagine; she knows the country very well. Her knowledge gives to the characters an intensive life and a warm coloring.

The origin of a faith analyzed with the help of true science is carried forward with great art beginning with the first thought which moves the heart of the Apostle, who loves mankind as He loves His family and His own country.

The author gives a vision, a revelation of all that is hidden of moving, precious depths in that supreme struggle. The liberating pain, the majesty of effort, the active bounty —all these elements of that struggle remain ordinarily unattainable for the crowd which cannot fathom under their austere dogmas, one of the beautiful forms of human unity.

The love, the deep necessity which lives in each human heart passes throughout the tragedy as an undercurrent, the fountainhead of which, never drying, remains hidden to the exterior world.

That beautiful and bold work points a return to the school of majesty and aesthetic morality, the aspiration to the eternal truth, which are the indelible character of permanent works. We foretell for this book a most merited success. Humanity, be it to its credit, is tired of the histories of the impure which spoil the taste and soil the mind. It cannot but receive with enthusiasm a work of which the most civilized countries of Europe will be proud.

Mrs. Grinevskaya, returning from Ramleh in January, 1911, gave interviews to the press at Odessa, the Russian port of the Black Sea, and as soon as she reached home she began her book, "A Journey to the Countries of the Sun," which is an account of her visit to 'Abdu'l-Bahá. This was interrupted because in the summer of 1912 she was called to Paris by the French translator of "Báb," Madame Halperin. When she came again to Leningrad she immediately began the publication of the drama "Bahá'u'lláh" so that it was not until 1914 that she completed the manuscript of "A Journey to the Countries of the Sun." It is interesting to note that when she completed it, three Iranians, Assad-Ullah Namdor of Moscow, 'Alí Akbar Kamalof of Táshkand and an old Iranian Bahá'í friend whom she had met at Port Said, came to call upon her and she read to them many parts from the "Journey," the central figure of which is 'Abdu'l-Bahá. This book of 550 pages has not yet been published because at this time the world war commenced; neither has it yet been translated into other languages.

May this great Russian poet, Mrs. Isabel Grinevskaya, who has made such a cultural contribution to literature and to the Bahá'í Movement someday see all her works translated into European languages! The English reading world eagerly awaits them, I know, for many inquiries come from the United States asking where it is possible to get these books in Russian, in French, or in German!

Appendix IV

The Ali and Nino Walking Tour

Extract from Betty Blair and Fuad Akhundow's "The Ali and Nino Walking Tour," containing an imaginary scene from the novel "Ali and Nino" in which the "oil barons" are depicted as engaging in a discussion on current affairs, with Naghiyev, the "Bahaist," representing the Bahá'í point of view

Musa Naghiyev features predominately in a scene in *Ali & Nino* when the most influential oil barons gather to meet with Ali's Father in their home on Kichik Gala Street in the Old City.

Other historic figures who attended this meeting in the novel include: Taghiyev (1823–1924), Ashurbeyli, and Asadullayev. The narrator of the novel dubs this group as "The Assembly of 'One Thousand Million Rubles' [1,000,000,000 or 1 billion rubles]." Naghiyev's building is directly on the opposite side of the wall of the citadel from Ali's home. In the novel, Naghiyev's statements are viewed as the most profound expressed that night.

Extremely worried about the deteriorating political scene, the millionaires wonder what the future holds and what will become of them. Little did they know that the Bolshevik occupation of their land in 1920 would bring an absolute end to their entrepreneurial capitalist activity for more than seventy years. In most cases, those who did not flee to neighboring countries were assassinated or imprisoned. Only in late 1991 when the Soviet Union collapsed, did Azerbaijan regain its independence and once again the entrepreneurial began to revive. . . .

* * *

From "Ali & Nino": Now Musa Naghi, the Bahaist, spoke: "I am an old man," he said, "and I am sad to see what I see, and to hear what I hear. The

135

Russians are killing the Turks, the Turks are killing the Armenians, the Armenians would like to kill us, and we the Russians. Is this good? I do not know.

We have heard what Zeynal Agha, Mirza, Ali and Fathali think of our people's fate. I understand they care deeply about schools, our language, hospitals and freedom. But what use is a school when what is taught there is nonsense, and what use is a hospital if it is the body only that is healed there, and the soul is forgotten? Our soul strives to go to God. But each nation believes they have God all to themselves, and He is the One and only God. But I believe it is the same God who made Himself known through the voices of all sages. Therefore, I worship Christ and Confucius, Buddha and Mohammad. We all come from one God, and through Bab, we shall all return to Him.

Men should be told that there is no Black and no White, for Black is White and White is Black. So my advice is this: let us not do anything that might hurt anybody anywhere in the world, for we are part of each soul, and each soul is part of us." We sat silent, nonplussed. So this was the heresy of Bab. Suddenly I heard loud sobbing, turned round and saw Asadulla, his face bathed in tears, and distorted with grief.

"Oh my soul!" he sobbed, "How right you are! What happiness to hear your words! O Almighty God! If only all men could find wisdom as profound as yours!" Then he dried his tears, sighed deeply and added, noticeably cooler: "Doubtlessly, venerated sir, the hand of God is above all our hands but, nevertheless, Oh, fountain of wisdom, the truth is, that one cannot always depend on the Almighty's merciful intervention. We are but men, and if inspiration fails, we have to find ways to overcome our difficulties." It was a clever sentence, as clever as his tears had been. Mirza was looking at his brother, full of admiration. The guests rose. Slender hands touched dark rows, saluting. Backs bent low, lips murmured; "Peace be with you. May the smile remain on your lips, friend."

The meeting was over. The "Thousand Million Rubles" went out into the street and parted, nodding, saluting, shaking hands. It was half past ten. The hall was empty and depressing. I felt very lonely.'"—Betty Blair and Fuad Akhundow, *The Ali and Nino Walking Tour*, from the website Azerbaijan International

Notes

Biography of Mírzá 'Alí-Akbar-i-Nakhjávání

1. As per the Wikipedia article on Baku: https://en.wikipedia.org/wiki/Baku.
2. Qur'án 38:25, 12:50.
3. Ishráq-Khavarí, *Rahíq-i-Makhtum*, vol. 2, pp. 309–10 (Translated from the Persian).
4. Ibid.
5. Ibid.
6. Ibid.
7. Marzieh Gail, *Summon Up Remembrance*, p. 102.
8. From notes of Ishráq-Khávarí.
9. From the Memoirs of 'Azízulláh Ázízí.
10. Hossain Moghbelpour, *Visit to Azerbijan and Georgia*.
11. Moojan Momen, *The Bábí and Bahá'í Religions, 1844–1944*, p. 50.
12. Ibid., p. 51.
13. Shoghi Effendi, *God Passes By*, p. 56.
14. *Star of the West*, vol. 24, Issue 1.
15. Ibid.
16. Ibid.
17. Moojan Momen, *The Bábí and Bahá'í Religions, 1844–1944*, p. 55.
18. 'Abdu'l-Bahá, *Selections from the Writings of 'Abdu'l-Bahá*, pp. 283–95.
19. Luigi Stendardo, *Leo Tolstoy and the Bahá'í Faith*, p. 49.
20. *Masábíh-i-Hidáyat*, vol. 7, under the biography of Jináb-i-Jazzáb, p. 495
21. Leo Tolstoy, *Polnoe Sobranie Sochnineii*, vol. LXXX, p.103.
22. Extract from a translation of a letter of Isabella Grinevskaya regarding her anticipated visit to the Holy Land in *Star of the West*, vol. 1, Issue 19, March 2, 1911, pp. 5–6.
23. Maḥmúd-i-Zarqání, *Mahmúd's Diary*, p. 124
24. Ibid., pp.115, 172.
25. References in Alan Ward, *239 days*, p. 146.

26. *Star of the West*, vol. 4, Issue 9, Aug 20, 1913.
27. Letter of F. K. Cheyne, Oxford, 1913 to 'Abdu'l-Bahá in *Star of the West*, vol 4, Issue 17, Jan 19, 1914.
28. *Star of the West*, vol. 5, Issue 1, March 21, 1914.
29. Aḥmad Sohrab to Harriet Magee, 1 June 1913.
30. Mírzá 'Alí-Akbar-i-Nakhjavání in Paris, based on Aḥmad Sohrab's letters. From Jan T. Jasion, *'Abdu'l-Baha in France*, (forthcoming).
31. Letters of Ḥájí Mírzá Ḥaydar-'Alí Isfahání to Mírzá Álí Akbar-i-Nakhjavání.
32. See: https://en.wikipedia.org/wiki/March_Days.
33. Shualan.
34. Faḍil Mazandarani, *Zuhu'ru'l-Haq* (vol. 8, p. 877).

Tablets and Letters addressed to Mírzá 'Alí-Akbar-i-Nakhjavání and other believers in Bákú

Item 1
Facsimile of original can be found on p. 69.
1. Áqá Músá Naqíov.
2. In allusion to Qur'án 54:55.

Item 2
Facsimile of original can be found on p. 70.
1. Sargis Mubagajian ("Atrpet").

Item 3
Facsimile of original can be found on p. 71.
1. Sargis Mubagajian.

Item 4
Facsimile of original can be found on p. 72.
1. Presumably Shaykh 'Alí-Akbar-i-Qúchání.

Item 5
Facsimile of original can be found on p. 73.
1. Probably Isabella Grinevskaya.

ITEM 6
Facsimile of original can be found on p. 74.
1. The quotation alludes to a famous ode of Ḥáfiẓ.
2. Olga Sergeyevna Lebedeva.

ITEM 7
Facsimile of original can be found on p. 75.
1. Karbilá'í Áqá Kishíy-i-'Alíov.
2. Ustád Áqá Bálá Karímov.
3. Sargis Mubagajian.
4. Presumably Shaykh 'Alí-Akbar-i-Qúchání.
5. Olga Sergeyevna Lebedeva.
6. Isabella Grinevskaya.

ITEM 8
Facsimile of original can be found on p. 76.
1. Professor E. G. Browne.
2. The Caucasus, identified with the fabled Mount Qáf, was the reputed
   home of the phoenix.
3. Ganja, Azerbaijan's second largest city.
4. The intention is perhaps the city of Shusha.

ITEM 9
Facsimile of original can be found on p. 77.

ITEM 10
Facsimile of original can be found on p. 78.

ITEM 11
Facsimile of original can be found on p. 79.

ITEM 12
Facsimile of original can be found on p. 80.
1. Referring perhaps to one of the Ahmadov brothers, sons of Ḥájí Aḥmad-
   i-Mílání, who were resident in Tbilisi.

ITEM 13

Facsimile of original can be found on p. 81.

1. The daughter of Bahá'u'lláh's third wife, Gawhar Khánum.
2. The daughter of Bahá'u'lláh's second wife, Mahd-i-'Ulyá.
3. Navváb.
4. *A Traveller's Narrative Written to Illustrate the Episode of the Báb*, translated by E. G. Browne.
5. Epistle to the Son of the Wolf.
6. Presumably, Shaykh 'Alí-Akbar-i-Qúchání.

ITEM 14

Facsimile of original can be found on p. 82.

1. Probably *Hujaj'ul Beheyyeh (The Behai Proofs)*, translated by Ali Kuli Khan (New York: J. W. Pratt & Co., 1902).
2. Hippolyte Dreyfus-Barney.
3. Probably Isabella Grinevskaya.
4. A Tablet of 'Abdu'l-Bahá known as the Lawh-i-Sharq va Gharb (The Tablet of East and West, *Makátíb-i-Hadrat-i-'Abdu'l-Bahá*, vol. 1, pp. 307–24).

ITEM 15

Facsimile of original can be found on p. 83.

1. Áqá Mírzá Muhsin Afnán.
2. A piece of land in Haifa which was bought in the name of Mírzá 'Alí-Akbar.
3. The one intended may be the martyr Shaykh 'Alí-Akbar-i-Qúchání, who, in 1327 A.H. (1909 A.D.), was directed by 'Abdu'l-Bahá to take up residence in Bákú in order to nurture its burgeoning Bahá'í community.

ITEM 16

Facsimile of original can be found on p. 84.

1. Probably Sargis Mubagajian.

ITEM 17

Facsimile of original can be found on p. 85.

1. Projected for Bákú. Áqá Músá Naqíov had volunteered, with the approval of the Master, to build a House of Worship in Bákú.

2. "Mahallu'l-Barakih" (literally "The Place of Blessing") referred to a community enterprise created by the Bahá'ís in Iran for the purpose of setting up a fund that could be used, among other things, for assisting the poor and needy, the education of children, and the propagation of the Bahá'í Faith.
3. The term "service council" (*majlis-i-khidmat*) was employed at this time to denote a committee of an Assembly which would attend to all practical, functional matters and details of the Assembly, its meetings, or the organized gatherings of the friends.
4. Presumably Mírzá 'Abdu'l-Kháliq-i-Ya'qúbzádih.

ITEM 18
Facsimile of original can be found on p. 86.
1. Arabic maxim.

ITEM 19
Facsimile of original can be found on p. 87.

ITEM 20
Facsimile of original can be found on p. 88.
1. The Birthday of Bahá'u'lláh.

ITEM 21
Facsimile of original can be found on p. 89.

ITEM 22
Facsimile of original can be found on p. 90.

ITEM 23
Facsimile of original can be found on p. 91.
1. Isabella Grinevskaya.

ITEM 24
Facsimile of original can be found on p. 92.
1. Cf. Qur'án 2:201.

ITEM 25

Facsimile of original can be found on p. 93.

1. In the Bahá'í Writings, "sharing" (*muvását*) and "equality" (*musávát*) denote, respectively, preferring others to oneself, and treating them equally to oneself.
2. The wife of Mírzá 'Alí-Akbar-i-Na<u>kh</u>javání.

ITEM 26

Facsimile of original can be found on p. 94.

1. The opening Súrih of the Qur'án; in other words, they pay lip service to the memory of the deceased, over whom the Fátiḥih would be recited at the time of interment.

ITEM 27

Facsimile of original can be found on p. 95.

1. Dr. Ḍíyá'u'lláh Ba<u>gh</u>dádí.
2. Dr. Ḍíyá'u'lláh Ba<u>gh</u>dádí's wife, Zínat <u>Kh</u>ánum, the sister-in-law of Mírzá 'Alí-Akbar-i-Na<u>kh</u>javání.
3. The wife of Mírzá 'Alí-Akbar-i-Na<u>kh</u>javání, and elder sister of Zínat <u>Kh</u>ánum.

ITEM 28

Facsimile of original can be found on pp. 96–97.

1. See Qur'án, súrih 55.
2. 31 July 1921.

ITEM 32

1. Siyyid 'Abdu'l-Karím-i-Urdúbádí.

ITEM 33

1. See Qur'án 50:1.
2. A mythical flying creature of Persian legend, sometimes equated with the griffin or the phoenix.
3. Jalálu'd-Dín Rúmí.

ITEM 34

1. See Qur'án, 25:38 and 50:12.

Digest of information from I_sh_ráq-_Kh_ávarí's epitome of the history of the Bahá'í Faith in Bákú

Information in this section is taken from *Yád-Namiy-i-I_sh_ráq-_Kh_ávarí*, pp. 262–90.

1. Probably the same Áqá Kí_sh_í referred to in Item 7 of Tablets and Letters addressed to Mírzá 'Alí-Akbar-i-Na_kh_javání and other believers in Bákú.
2. An outlying village of the city of _Sh_írván, to the southwest of Bákú, in which Bahá'ís resided even at the time of Bahá'u'lláh.
3. The seat of the Salyán district, or raion, in the south-eastern Arán region of Azerbaijan.
4. As will be recorded, Mullá Abú-Ṭálib spent his final days in Haifa in the presence of 'Abdu'l-Bahá.
5. "Explicit orders had been issued by the Sulṭán and his ministers to subject the exiles, who were accused of having grievously erred and led others far astray, to the strictest confinement. Hopes were confidently expressed that the sentence of life-long imprisonment pronounced against them would lead to their eventual extermination. The farmán of Sulṭán 'Abdu'l-'Azíz, dated the fifth of Rabí'u'th-Thání 1285 A.H. (July 26, 1868), not only condemned them to perpetual banishment, but stipulated their strict incarceration, and forbade them to associate either with each other or with the local inhabitants. The text of the farmán itself was read publicly, soon after the arrival of the exiles, in the principal mosque of the city as a warning to the population. The Persian Ambassador, accredited to the Sublime Porte, had thus assured his government, in a letter, written a little over a year after their banishment to 'Akká: 'I have issued telegraphic and written instructions, forbidding that He (Bahá'u'lláh) associate with any one except His wives and children, or leave under any circumstances, the house wherein He is imprisoned. 'Abbás-Qulí Khán, the Consul-General in Damascus . . . I have, three days ago, sent back, instructing him to proceed direct to 'Akká . . . confer with its governor regarding all necessary measures for the strict maintenance of their imprisonment . . . and appoint, before his return to Damascus, a representative on the spot to insure that the orders issued by the Sublime Porte will, in no wise, be disobeyed. I have, likewise, instructed him that once every three months he should proceed from Damascus to 'Akká, and

personally watch over them, and submit his report to the Legation.' Such was the isolation imposed upon them that the Bahá'ís of Persia, perturbed by the rumors set afloat by the Azalís of Isfahán that Bahá'u'lláh had been drowned, induced the British Telegraph office in Julfá to ascertain on their behalf the truth of the matter."—Shoghi Effendi, *God Passes By*, p. 186

6. "Discourses": a compilation of the author's talks.

7. The foundation-stone of the Shrine of the Báb was laid by 'Abdu'l-Bahá sometime in 1899, following the arrival of the Báb's remains in the Holy Land on January 31 of that same year.

8. "*Bravo, respected Ashraf, well done, well done!*"

9. The former is the single (unused) door on the northern side (front) of the structure, which overlooks the Bay of Haifa, while the latter is what is now the central door on its eastern side.

10. As mentioned above, 'Abdu'l-Bahá, in a Tablet to Ustád Bálá, addresses him: "O Bálá! Thou art called by all 'Bálá' ('Exalted'); yet I for my part call thee 'balá' ('calamity'), inasmuch as thou art a calamity unto the enemies of the Cause of His Holiness the All-Merciful."

11. i.e., consequent upon the Bolshevik Revolution of October 1917.

12. In other words, the Master did not interfere with the electoral process, but merely appointed Ustád Bálá as an "*ex officio*" member of the elected body on His, 'Abdu'l-Bahá's, behalf.

13. "O MY FRIENDS! Walk ye in the ways of the good pleasure of the Friend, and know that His pleasure is in the pleasure of His creatures."—Bahá'u'lláh, the Hidden Words, Persian, no. 43.

14. Implying that the Master had granted Ustád Bálá's request to be relieved of membership of the Spiritual Assembly of Bákú.

15. In other words, the Master's purpose had been not so much to affect the result of the election, as to repair the damage done to Ustád Bálá's reputation by the campaign of defamation against him.

16. The Hajinskis were an important family of Bákú, whose members included various prominent figures, such as the administrator and architect Mammad Hasan Hajinski; the publicist and patron of the arts Jamo Bey Hajinski; and the "oil baron" Isa Bey Hajinski, who constructed the "House of Hajinsky."

17. i.e., Hájí Abu'l-Hasan-i-Ardikání, the second Trustee of Ḥuqúqu'lláh (see a previous note).

18. Ḥájí Abu'l-Ḥasan, who, as previously noted, had, by virtue of his role as Trustee of Ḥuqúqu'lláh, been surnamed "Amín-i-Iláhí" ("Divine Trustee"), was better known among the friends as "Ḥájí Amín."

19. i.e., the Shrine of Bahá'u'lláh in Bahjí.

20. This beautiful building was modeled on the Doge's Palace in Venice.

21. Shamsi Asadullayev (1840–1913) "was an Azerbaijani national oil baron and philanthropist. He was the first businessman to use barges as transportation means to export oil out of Baku."—Wikipedia article "Shamsi Asadullayev"

22. "The Armenian–Azerbaijani War, which started after the Russian Revolution, was a series of brutal and hard-to-classify conflicts in 1918, then from 1920 to 1922, that occurred during the brief independence of Armenia and Azerbaijan and afterwards. Most of the conflicts did not have a principal pattern with a standard armed structure."—Wikipedia article "Armenian-Azerbaijani War"

23. Mirza Alakbar Sabir (1862–1911) "was an Azerbaijani satirical poet, public figure, philosopher and teacher. He set up an inspiring attitude to classical traditions, rejecting well-trodden ways in poetry. Never before did the people's attitude to the world, the voice of Azerbaijani people find so splendid and complete an embodiment, devoid of stylization, as in Sabir's writings."—Wikipedia article "Mirza Alakbar Sábir." In fact, the Ismailiyya Palace now houses the Azerbaijan National Academy of Sciences.

24. The figure appears to be an error for a much smaller number in the region of the hundreds (say, 250): "The fourth meeting of Muslims for the Society for promoting literacy, Nasr-Muarif, was held at the Public Assembly hall on 15 February 1913. The event featured passages from Shevlyanov's comedy, 'A Day from the Life of a Dead Man,' the opera Shah Abbas and the operetta, the Husband and the Wife. Kovsar Asadullayeva, the daughter of the head of the City Assembly, Mirza Samsi Asadullayev, and Rugiya Nagiyeva, the niece of Musa Nagiyev, were selling souvenirs in special kiosks. A charity dinner was organized by the wives of prominent figures—A. Asurova, S. Hasanova, E. M. Nazanskaya, L. Muxtarova and others. The event was attended by Baku governor, Alisevskiy, Baku police chief, Nazanskiy, and other officials. The event gathered about 8,000 rubles. Tagiyev's contribution was 1,000 rubles. Other well-known oil businessmen—

Aga Samsi Asadullayev and Aga Musa Nagiyev—followed Tagiyev's example. Asadullayev had a large house in Moscow in which a madrasah was located. He said that in spring he would start building a four-story house there and 150,000 rubles were allocated for the construction. The entire profit from the construction would go for the expansion of a primary school. At the time the school had four departments and 56 students. The school had a boarding institution to accommodate poor children. The most generous donation however came from Aga Musa Nagiyev. He turned to the Baku city Assembly with a proposal to build and equip a new surgery hospital (which currently bears Nagiyev's name) for 225 beds which would meet modern standards. Nagiyev promised to transfer about 300,000 to the city budget on condition that the city authorities would build the hospital within three years. The benefactor also expressed the desire to detach 50 beds out of the 225 and specially design them for Muslim women in accordance with their lifestyle. Members of the city council accepted Nagiyev's gift with gratefulness and unanimously decided to feature his portrait in the future hospital. They also decided to name one of the streets the hospital would face after Nagiyev. The new hospital was to be built in Samaxinka. The city administration allocated a site at the corner of two boulevards—Staroselskiy and Aleksandriyskiy."— Mirabbas Mammadov, Baku, May 20, 2013, from the website "Regionplus"

25. Meshadi Azizbekov (1876–1918) "was a legendary Soviet revolutionary of Azerbaijani origin, leader of the revolutionary movement in Azerbaijan, one of the first Azeri Marxists, Provincial Commissioner and Deputy People's Commissar of Internal Affairs, gubernial commissar for Baku. He was one of the 26 Baku Commissars."—Wikipedia article "Meshadi Azizbekov." In fact, the hospital appears to have been renamed again, in commemoration of its founder, as the Musa Nagiyev Clinical Hospital.

26. Nariman Narimanov (1870–1925) "was an Azerbaijani revolutionary, writer, publicist, politician, and statesman."—Wikipedia article "Nariman Narimanov"

27. i.e., again, Ḥájí Abu'l-Ḥasan-i-Ardikání, the second Trustee of Ḥuqúqu'lláh (see above).

28. In other words, the portion of his property payable to the Center of the Faith as Ḥuqúqu'lláh.
29. In confirmation of which, in the Wikipedia article "Músá Naghiyev," the final item of information provided about the subject before the record of his decease on 4 March 1919, is that "He was also an adherent of the Bahá'í Faith and served on the Local Spiritual Assembly of the Bahá'ís of Baku."
30. Zeynalabdin Taghiyev (1821 / 1823 / 1838–1924) "was an Azeri national industrial magnate and philanthropist."—Wikipedia article "Zeynalabdin Taghiyev"
31. A type of Russian carriage of the time.
32. "The Müsavat (Equality) Party (Azerbaijani: Müsavat Partiyası) (Arabic (مساواة) 'equality, parity') is the oldest existing political party in Azerbaijan. Its history can be divided into three periods: Early (old) Musavat, Musavat-in-exile and New Musavat."—Wikipedia article "Musavat"

Article by Martha L. Root entitled "Russia's Cultural Contribution to the Bahá'í Faith," published in "The Bahá'í World," vol. VI, pp. 707–12

1. Pamphlets in French and English, London, 1907, at the Press of "Chronide," 29, Besborough [*sic*] Street, London, S.W.
2. The intention is undoubtedly 'Alí-Akbar-i-Na<u>kh</u>javání. According to the current transliteration system, the name "Mame<u>dh</u>anly" would read: "Muhammad-<u>Kh</u>ánli." It is a Turkish and Azeri practice to change the sound "<u>kh</u>" to "h." For example, the Turks and Azeris, instead of saying "<u>Kh</u>ánum," as is the practice in Bahá'í circles, have the habit of pronouncing it as "Hánum" (because the sound "<u>kh</u>" is considered by them to be harsh and indelicate. There are other such conventions, namely: "b" is pronounced as "p;" likewise "d" is preferably pronounced as "t," or entirely dropped, etc.)
3. In a footnote Mrs. Grinevskaya adds that her utmost desire, which she had expressed in Ramleh, had been that her poems might be translated into European languages. The poem "The Báb" has been translated into German and French, but the poem "Bahá'u'lláh" is still untranslated.

Mírzá 'Alí-Akbar-i-Na<u>kh</u>javání as a young man, exact date unknown.

Mírzá ‘Alí-Akbar-i-Na<u>kh</u>javání while performing his
duties as executive secretary of Mírzá Músa Naqíov,
exact date unknown.

Mírzá 'Alí-Akbar-i-Nakhjavání, holding a photograph of 'Abdu'l-Bahá, in the company of a group of Bahá'í friends in 'Ishqábád, exact date unknown.

Mírzá 'Alí-Akbar, holding hands with an unidentified young couple in Green Acre, 1912.

A fleeting glimpse of Mírzá 'Alí-Akbar, walking behind 'Abdu'l-Bahá
during His visit to America.

Standing with 'Abdu'l-Bahá and His entourage on Riverside Drive
in New York. Mírzá 'Alí-Akbar-i-Na<u>kh</u>javání is standing second from the left.

'Abdu'l-Bahá with a few of the Bahá'ís attending the Unity Feast
at Roy Wilhelm's home in West Englewood. Mírzá 'Alí-Akbar-i-Na<u>kh</u>javání
is seated in the front left.

Visit to Mr. Topakyan, Persian Consul General, at Morristown, New Jersey, June 20, 1912. Mírzá 'Alí-Akbar-i-Na<u>kh</u>javání is standing on the steps, third from the bottom on the right.

At a luncheon given in honor of 'Abdu'l-Bahá by Consul General Topakyan.
Mírzá 'Alí-Akbar-i-Na<u>kh</u>javání is seated directly in front
with his left shoulder to the camera.

Photograph taken of 'Abdu'l-Bahá with His entourage by Elize Cabot
on August 15, 1912 on the lawn of the Parsons' home.
Mírzá 'Alí-Akbar is standing third from the left.

'Abdu'l-Bahá at Green Acre. Mírzá 'Alí-Akbar-i-Na<u>kh</u>javání
is standing behind the Master, third from the left.

'Abdu'l-Bahá speaking to Sarah Farmer.
Mírzá 'Alí-Akbar is the first on the left.

In St. Paul, Minneapolis. Mírzá 'Alí-Akbar-i-Nakhjavání is the fourth from the right, standing behind 'Abdu'l-Bahá's bench.

'Abdu'l-Bahá and His entourage on the main drive, Leland Stanford Junior University, Palo Alto, California, following His address on October 8, 1912. Mírzá 'Alí-Akbar is standing behind the Master, second from the right.

'Abdu'l-Bahá at the children's meeting at Mrs. Goodall's home in Oakland, California. Mírzá 'Alí-Akbar is standing immediately behind the Master, the fourth from the right.

'Abdu'l-Bahá meeting Bahá'ís in the grounds of Mrs. Goodall's home in Oakland, California. Mírzá 'Alí-Akbar is standing in the back row, immediately behind and to the left of 'Abdu'l-Bahá.

Members of Mírzá 'Alí-Akbar-i-Na<u>kh</u>javání's immediate family, circa 1920.

Left to right, back row: Mírzá Áqá Urujov, brother-in-law of Mírzá 'Alí-Akbar. Middle row: Izzat Urujova, niece of Mírzá 'Alí-Akbar; Rubabih Urujova, sister of Mírzá 'Alí-Akbar; Ali Nakhjavani, youngest son of Mírzá 'Alí-Akbar; Fáṭimih <u>Kh</u>ánum, widow of Mírzá 'Alí-Akbar; three persons unknown.

Front row: Munib Urujov, nephew of Mírzá 'Alí-Akbar; Jalal Nakhjavani, eldest son of Mírzá 'Alí-Akbar.

Fáṭimih <u>Kh</u>ánum, the widow of Mírzá ʿAlí-Akbar, fleeing from Bákú
in the wake of the Bolshevik Revolution, circa 1920.

Fáṭimih <u>Kh</u>ánum, the widow of Mírzá ʿAlí-Akbar, in Haifa,
some years prior to her departure for Iran.

The grave of Mírzá 'Alí-Akbar-i-Na<u>kh</u>javání in the main cemetery of Bákú.
Although he passed away in his summer residence of Shualan, his sister Rubabih
later transferred his remains to the capital and replaced his gravestone,
during the Stalin period, with one using Cyrillic lettering.